Congratul
bach-to-back medal.

You are a true Winged
Messenger!

Best wish

B F
2403

Alfred J Robinson

10 September 2024

To Claire and Joe

Congratulations on being
a winged messenger
and a back-to-back
Comrades medallist

Best wishes

B T
2403

WINGED MESSENGER

RUNNING YOUR FIRST COMRADES MARATHON

BRUCE FORDYCE

Winged Messenger

© Bruce Fordyce 2021

ISBN:
978-1-77605-681-1 (Paperback)
978-1-77605-680-4 (eBook)

Editing: Anine Vorster
Cover Design: Anita Stander
Design and Typeset: Janet von Kleist-Klein

Printed in South Africa
Published by Kwarts Publishers
www.kwartspublishers.co.za

Website: www.brucefordyce.com
E-mail: bruce@brucefordyce.com
Facebook: BruceFordycerun
Twitter: @BruceFordycerun
Instagram: bruce_fordyce

"There is only one runner that has completely understood the totality of the demands that it takes to win the Comrades Marathon consistently for more than a decade. How he began to understand those demands is described uniquely in these pages."

-*Tim Noakes*

Dedication

On my mantlepiece rests a miniature First World War burial shroud. Over 72 000 miniature shrouds were commissioned to commemorate soldiers from the British Commonwealth, whose names are recorded at Thiepval Memorial, where they are listed as missing, presumed dead. The shroud was a gift from my sister, Oonagh, who understands my love of military history and like me, admires and misses our father Noel, who was himself a soldier in the 2nd King Edward VII's Own Gurkha Rifles. This shroud commemorates Serjeant George Edward Piggins of the Cambridgeshire Regiment who died at the battle of the Somme in 1916 at the age of 22. Serjeant Piggins was one of 20 000 British and Commonwealth soldiers who fell on the first day of the battle. At the battle's end in November 1916, over one million soldiers on both sides of the conflict had been killed or wounded or were missing in battle. The shroud reminds me that Vic Clapham started the Comrades Marathon to commemorate the bravery, dedication, stamina and comradeship of his colleagues in the First World War. This book is therefore also dedicated to the fallen of all conflicts.

This book is dedicated to every Comrades Marathon novice runner embarking on one of life's great adventures, and in particular, to those who have stumbled on their journey, like my friend Ulrike Karg, whose Comrades dream has been cruelly deferred three times. I sincerely hope it helps novices to better understand the great odyssey that is the Comrades Marathon and that it helps many of you to become "winged messengers".

The emblem of Hermes on the Comrades badge.

The distinctive emblem embossed on every Comrades Marathon medal is that of the Greek god Hermes. Hermes, whose Roman counterpart was Mercury, was the winged messenger of the Olympian gods and appropriately was also the god of the roads and travellers. In his arms, Hermes carried a Kerykeion (Latin translation: *caduceus*) as his messenger symbol. Today the men's and women's winners are presented with a caduceus as they cross the finish line. Most importantly, Hermes was the only god who could move freely between the underworld (Hades) and the realm of the living. While running the Comrades Marathon, every runner also moves from the old world to the new and is reborn as a new and different person. Like Hermes, Comrades runners become winged messengers.

With about 30 kilometres left to run in the Comrades Marathon, you suddenly meet someone you deeply admire and respect, and that person is yourself.

Acknowledgements

My parents, for their wonderful support and their unstinting belief in me, and for their winning genes!

My stepfather, Roly, for his wisdom and advice and his companionship on some of those early long runs.

My Wits University teammates, for their encouragement and friendship on the road. I cannot think of a running club of which I have been prouder to be a member. As the university approaches its centenary year, I am delighted to boast that I once proudly wore its blue and gold colours.

The Comrades Marathon Association and everyone connected with this great race, and especially Vic Clapham whose gift to South Africa and the world was this unique race.

Alan Robb, for his insightful piece in this guide on his experience of the 1977 Comrades. But also, for his inspiration, his intense rivalry on the road between Durban and Pietermaritzburg, and most importantly, for his friendship.

Tim Noakes for his friendship and the overly generous foreword he wrote for this book.

My loyal seconds and friends, who despite some verbal abuse and prima donna behaviour on the road continued to encourage, motivate, and bully me into achieving my dream.

My family, for their long-suffering patience, while this project, at times, stuttered along, and for their advice and encouragement when every I stalled at a literary Polly Shortts.

I must also recognise my wife Gill's understanding and compassion about a time in my life when we were yet to meet.

The team from Kwarts Publishers, for their kind support and guidance with this project.

Wedding anniversary celebration with my wife Gill.

Contents

Foreword

Bruce Fordyce is the single most important reason why running, especially ultramarathon running – a sport considered peculiar in the rest of the world – is a mainstream sport in South Africa. Between 1981 and 1990, he achieved the impossible: Winning the nine Comrades Marathons in a row that he entered, eclipsing by a total of four – the highest number of wins recorded by all the legendary Comrades runners who had preceded him.

Paradoxically, his achievement devalued his achievement because, if he had not ever achieved it, we would have known for sure that it is an impossible feat. But once he achieved it, we suddenly wondered why we ever thought it was impossible. The truth is that, as a winner of the Comrades Marathon, Bruce Fordyce will always stand alone. His achievement will never be repeated. I say this with conviction because Bruce's achievement was not because he was lucky or uniquely gifted, or because his competition was "weak". He won consistently because he perfected the way he prepared his body and his mind for what he wanted to achieve. He did this because he has a unique ability to understand how his body and mind respond to everything he asks of them. And he moderates his training, either more or less, accordingly. For more than a decade, he also knew precisely how fit he needed to be on every single day of every year if he was to win the next Comrades Marathon. And then on race day, he ran with the same methodical certainty and exquisite pacing for just under the five hours and thirty minutes that made him invincible.

Finally, he fell in love with the course on which the race is run. He knows every inch of the road – every uphill, every downhill, the most economical line through every turn, when to speed up, when to hold back – as if it is just another of his favourite training courses in his home town.

In time his acclaim, not just for his unique achievement but also for the warm, vibrant, engaging, utterly unassuming and overwhelmingly positive person that he is spread across South Africa and the world. And so he became the widely loved and respected South African icon that he is today. But there was a time in June 1976 when all this lay ahead of him, when Bruce was just another university student struggling to find direction in an uncertain, complex and divided nation. No one, and least of all himself, could ever in their wildest of predictions have imagined what lay ahead, how Bruce would make his unique contribution to South African sport in general, global ultramarathon running in particular. That is what makes this book so gripping. It takes us back to the beginning of an achievement that no one saw coming. Here we are privileged to share the road with Bruce as he begins his quest on June 8, 1976, not to win the Comrades, but simply to become just a little fitter.

We learn that his first run lasted just ten minutes and included a long walk. Not so different from the original Comrades Marathon legend and five-times winner, Arthur Newton, whose first training run on January 1, 1922, was a little further (three kilometres) than Bruce's, but which left him so stiff that he was unable to run for two days. Twenty weeks later, Newton won the second running of the Comrades Marathon in eight hours and forty minutes. How will Bruce fare by comparison, we wonder?

We then follow Bruce's daily progression. In his first month of training, he runs 178 kilometres, including one day in which he runs twice. He is starting to run faster. By December 1976, he is running more than 200 kilometres per week and progressively increasing his speed. He is now running at a pace of three minutes and fifty seconds per kilometre, and this at altitude.

A key moment happens on February 8, 1977, when he joins the University of Witwatersrand Athletics Club and acquires mentors who are experienced Comrades Marathon runners. Importantly, he discovers that he is able to keep pace with all and even outrun some of these veterans. On February 13, he runs 34 kilometres in a single run, a landmark for any runner. A week later he runs his first competitive race, the Springs Striders 32-kilometre event with 1 300 other runners. This would have been a HUGE race in those days; the dramatic increase in long-distance/marathon running was only just beginning. Remarkably, he runs the first 16 kilometres in less than an hour, slowing in the second half to finish 103rd in two hours and five minutes. Clearly, the boy has some talent!

But he is already learning. He learns that he started far too fast. He would not make that mistake again. By now he is committed to running the 1977 Comrades Marathon with just one goal: Finishing.

A month later he enters and completes his first 42-kilometre marathon, finishing 24th in 02:44:54. Learning from his first race, he "starts like a coward and finishes like a hero". It will become the trademark of how he races. His total mileage for March is 359 kilometres. He is beginning to realise that the time to do the intensive training for the Comrades is March, April and early May. Not January, February, March, April and May.

On April 24, he finishes the 53.5-kilometre Pieter Korkie Marathon in three hours and thirty-eight minutes in 30th position, earning his first silver medal for finishing in under four hours. And then on May 31, he achieves his goal, finishing the Comrades Marathon in six hours and forty-five minutes in 43rd place, earning a silver medal and firmly setting him on the road to becoming a serious athlete.

This book is just another stellar contribution that Bruce has made in promoting his joy of running and especially of completing the ultimate ultramarathon challenge for all levels of runners: The Comrades Marathon. May reading it inspire you to dream big and to follow the path that he has forged for the rest of us to follow – each in our own special way. But know that there is only one runner in its history that has completely understood the totality of the demands that it takes to win the Comrades Marathon consistently for more than a decade. How he began to understand those demands is described uniquely in these pages.

Tim Noakes
October 2020

Tim Noakes, renowned scientist, sports
medicine practitioner, and marathoner, running
the Two Oceans Marathon in the 1980s.

Introduction

In the months that it has taken me to write this guide for
Comrades novices, I have had the pleasure of travelling
on two journeys. The first was the journey of writing the
book itself. At times I hit mental roadblocks like running
into the base of Inchanga Mountain or that nasty unnamed
hill outside Camperdown village. At other times I sped
along as if I were turning at the corner of Washington Road
on the "up" run and speeding past the traffic lights into the
crowd lined Oribi Road while smiling and waving at the
spectators. The other journey was the sometimes delightful, sometimes nostalgic, and at other times sad journey
back to another time, another place when the world was a
different planet and South Africa a very different country
and I, a very young Wits student, harboured a dream of
running South Africa's most famous race. I hope you, the
reader, will forgive me the self-indulgence at times and
the far too frequent use of the first person singular in this
book, but if I am to give an account of the journey to the
starting line of my first Comrades Marathon while also

hoping to impart some knowledge, I have no choice. I also hope that you, the aspiring Comrades runner, will gain some valuable insights into the journey that lies ahead of you. In this book, I have recorded the training that I undertook in order to run the Comrades, but I have also tried to place my journey into the context of my own young life at that time and also into the context of the troubled country that South Africa was back then in the 1970s. It is impossible to divorce these important influences from the task of training for a Comrades Marathon. To both steal and twist a famous quote from John Lennon, a hero of mine: "Life is what happens to you while you're busy making Comrades plans."

This is particularly apt now as I sit and write in the middle of the 2020 Covid-19-pandemic. Thousands of Comrades runners have no idea when they will next run a Comrades. Thousands have had to put their Comrades plans on hold. Life, or rather fearmongering in the form of Covid-19, has stopped us in mid-stride. In South Africa, we are facing a particularly draconian and, in my opinion, unnecessarily harsh lockdown, where, at times, we have been prevented from running outside our own homes. We do not just long for the Comrades; we long to run properly. But I take comfort from the words of another Beatle, George Harrison: "All things must pass" and this time will end, and we will gather again in our thousands in Pietermaritzburg and Durban, and we will hear Max Trimborn's echoing cockerel crow again.

Back in the late 1970s, the Comrades Marathon was a very different race from the one it is today. For most of its history, the race had always been exclusively a white adult male event. A mere two years before I ran my first Comrades, the race was finally opened to include black runners and also women. Indeed, in my first Comrades Marathon, there were only two black runners ahead of me at the finish and only four in the first hundred finishers. Lettie van Zyl was one of a handful of women runners, and she won the race in just under nine hours. Apart from a handful of Zimbabweans (Rhodesians back then), I do not recall any foreign runners in the race. The last foreign winner of the race was Mick Orton from England who had won in 1972. The next would be Germany's Charly Doll in 1993.

South Africa was in a different lockdown back then, crushed by the vice-like grip of the apartheid Nationalist regime and as a result, excluded from international sport and alienated by the rest of the world. Despite apartheid appearing to be fully entrenched, the cracks were beginning to show and the tumultuous events of June 16, 1976, was one of the spurs for the birth of my own running journey. A few months after my first run, the Black Consciousness Movement leader, Steve Biko, was murdered while being held in detention by security police. Both these horrendous events served to isolate South Africa further. This isolation forced South Africans to become more and more insular, and when it came to sport, South Africans looked inwards and followed our own national events. Though it still had a long way to go to become the major international event, it is how the Comrades had started to grow in stature.

South Africans were first introduced to television in 1976, and in ensuing years, television coverage helped to boost the race. (Yes, we were one of the few nations on Earth whose citizens were not able to watch Neil Armstrong take his first steps on the Moon in July 1969.)

The clothes we students wore were a symbol of protest. Daily dress for me were jeans (often frayed and very faded) tie-dyed T-shirts, and grandpa vests. I always wore tan coloured veldskoens and occasionally headbands. Strangely, my music tastes were very Eurocentric and American. That was because it was the only music to which we were regularly exposed to. The social isolation of apartheid meant that white students were largely unaware of many of the brilliant local bands and musicians living almost on our doorsteps. I remember being aware of a talented South African musician called Johnny Clegg, and I had heard his band, Juluka, playing at one or two concerts. I also bumped into Johnny in the corridors of our university where he was studying social anthropology and I archaeology. At times, our two degrees intersected. However, I really loved the progressive rock music of bands like Pink Floyd, Led Zeppelin, Genesis, Yes and Jethro Tull. Many of the famous songs by these bands accompanied my training and racing in those days.

My sister Oonagh is one year younger than me and many years wiser and more sensible. She studied BA Drama at Wits. She is also far better looking than me. In 1976, she was crowned Wits Rag queen and led the annual rag procession through Johannesburg on a horse-drawn carriage accompanied by her two rag princesses. My contemporaries at Wits often teased me that I was sufficiently arrogant to believe that I had acquired some notoriety on the campus because I had won the Comrades marathon a few times in Wits colours. They assured me that I was famous at university because I was Oonagh's brother.

A typical day at university would consist of several lectures and some studying in the Wartenweiler Library or my residence room. Lunch was more often taken in the student canteen, which was a favoured gathering place for all undergraduate students. Slap (sloppy) chips and gravy was a staple meal, especially for those of us whose funds were running low.

Most of my training in the week was completed in the afternoon or early evening and on the weekends in the early morning. In the early days, I trained almost entirely on my own, but as the Comrades became a reality and the 1977 academic year had begun, a great part of my training was done with my university club mates.

This morning while out running, I bumped into a young runner called Jess. (The Covid-19-lockdown has just been eased a little and we are now permitted to run in a short window of three hours.) As often happens with runners who meet on the road, we shared a couple of kilometres and chatted about running. Inevitably, the conversation turned to the subject of the Comrades Marathon.

"Have you run it, Jess?" I enquired.

"No," she answered emphatically, "it's too far for me and too tough. I prefer running ten kilometres and half-marathons."

And so we carried on silently running for a while and then she suddenly asked, "Is it a very emotional moment crossing the finish line at the Comrades?"

And with that query, I knew she is doomed, doomed in an exciting way, to embark on her own Comrades journey one day. There is no adventure quite like that of running your first Comrades Marathon. As is happening with my new friend Jess, it starts as a gentle enquiry, a nagging germ of an idea which is quickly stamped out by furious denial. But the idea refuses to go away, and it resurfaces and continues to niggle and grow until the point is reached where there can be no denying that the germ has grown into a monster, a reality.

"Ok, I'm going to attempt this ridiculous journey, but I'm not going to tell anyone in case I fail or change my mind."

But of course, no one can attempt a challenge like the Comrades Marathon without soliciting help. So, informing and including others in your dream is essential if the challenge is to be met.

This short guide is an attempt to help first-time Comrades runners like Jess and others to perhaps understand that we all have the same concerns and fears, that we all have nagging doubts, and we all dream that we will achieve the seemingly impossible. (Even future winners.) I hope that it is also proof that the seemingly impossible is possible. The Comrades journey is completely life-altering, and the challenge can be met.

In order to prove that assertion, I am going to document my own journey to my first Comrades Marathon finish. I will add notes outlining my mistakes, my worries and eventually, my success. I will write about my progress and the steps that need to be taken to climb the mountain that is the Comrades. The reader will have to understand that we all have vastly different athletic abilities, and these differences are genetically pre-determined. I chose my parents very carefully and wisely, and they created a son who is designed to run very quickly over exceptionally long distances. So, this genetic advantage enabled me to run a 06:45 first Comrades Marathon on a fairly low training base. Once I became serious about it all, two years later, the results were beyond the wildest dreams of the 1977 novice. However, the training principles apply to all of us, and I think many runners will find that my first Comrades adventure has lessons for us all, but particularly for novices. I made plenty of mistakes, and my notes will point them out, but in the end, I got it right, and I earned a silver medal at my first attempt.

My Comrades adventure began in June 1976 and from that first germ of an idea to that day in late May 1977 when I crossed the finish line in the Jan Smuts Stadium in Pietermaritzburg, slightly less than a calendar year had passed. Yes, it was an "up" run, and it was also a long time ago. Much has changed since then. There were barely 1 500 of us who finished that race. There were fewer running clubs, and there was no prize money, no live television coverage, no seeding, no international runners, and no pre-race expo. There was, however, a brutal 11-hour final cut-off gun and there were only three medals for which to strive: gold, silver and bronze.

There was mobile seconding. (Yes, our families and seconds could follow us along the entire route, screaming encouragement and handing us drinks from the car win-dow.) When my Wits teammate Derick Raal had a weak moment and believed he had had enough on the tough Harrison Flats stretch (65 km), he decided he wanted to bail (drop out) and climb into the car that was following him. His running companions instructed Derick's family to lock their car doors and drive ahead five kilometres. Five kilometres later, Derick changed his mind, and he ran on to eventually earn a silver medal.

In those early years, there were club war cries before the start, and it was possible to find friends at the start and wish them luck. Thanks to the 1974 British Lions rugby team who had thrashed our beloved South African Springboks, salt tablets were the latest craze. (The British Lions believed that salt tablets helped them combat the blazing African sun.) We all had to swallow lots of salt tablets! If salt tablets were the perceived friend of Comrades runners, dehydration was the enemy. We were all encouraged to drink lots, to drink often, and to drink in anticipation of dehydrating. We were warned, "If you feel thirsty, it's too late!" Tim Noakes hadn't yet written *Waterlogged*, highlighting the dangers of overhydration (hyponatremia). In fact, Tim probably drank as much fluid as the rest of us when he ran his seven Comrades Marathons.

But much has remained the same and most of the core traditions are still part of the race. Of course, nothing has altered the challenge of the race, and the sense of triumph and joy novice runners feel when they complete their first Comrades Marathon.

I suppose I had always harboured the virus that is the Comrades somewhere deep in my bones. The Comrades is as much a part of the DNA of South Africans as biltong and braaivleis, and I can remember it being a part of my life from early on, if only as a fascinated listener on the radio. It helped that athletics has always been my favourite sport and that the longer distances have always been my particular passion. My early heroes were the East African distance runners, and Kipchoge Keino, Naftali Temu, Ben Jipcho, Abebe Bikila and Mamo Wolde were runners who inspired me. I was a strong runner from an early age, and I also learnt that the longer the distance raced, the better I fared. At Woodmead School, I won the school cross-country, the 1 500 metres and 5 000 metres and *victor ludorum* in my senior year. In 1973, our school also staged a charity relay from Durban to Johannesburg, and I was one of the stronger runners in the team. But I was still concerned when I embarked on my Comrades journey that winning school races and running well in a charity relay were not clear indications that I could complete South Africa's gruelling Comrades Marathon. Like every novice Comrades runner, I was riddled with doubt. (Interestingly, the official starter of our school charity relay was the legendary Comrades runner, Ian Jardine. I often wish I had spent some time talking to him about the Comrades, but I was too busy preparing to run the second leg of the relay.)

Woodmead School athletics, 1974 – 5 000 metres.

We had a teacher who had run the Comrades, and we learnt that we could distract him from teaching some boring subject by asking him questions about the marathon. He would sound off enthusiastically and at length about the race, and we would miss many minutes of our dull lesson. But whereas my fellow scholars were simply glad to create a diversion, I listened with intense interest to all he had to say about the race. I have often wondered if he remembered the young boy who sat at the back of the class listening keenly to all he had to say and if he is aware now that that young boy would one day win the race. A few years later, I recall staring at a man who was wearing a Comrades Marathon blazer. I think we were in a shop somewhere and his blazer badge, with its distinct Hermes motif, inspired me. Every Republic Day, I would huddle around our family radio and listen to early broadcasts of races won by my heroes Dave Bagshaw, Mick Orton, and Dave Levick. I remember watching the first televised programme of the race in 1976. (As I mentioned earlier, television was only introduced to South Africans in 1976.) Even then that broadcast was not live but was produced as a half an hour summary of the race and shown a fortnight after race day. I watched Alan Robb win his first Comrades after a tussle with Great Britain's Cavin Woodward. But it wasn't Alan's great run that inspired me (as far as I was concerned the race winner was a different species from me, a running god or perhaps even some strange alien), but rather the mere mortals at the back of the field. Some of them were clearly not athletically gifted and yet they battled across the line. I remember thinking that if this chubby, unathletic bloke can do it, then surely I can too.

However, after two years as a student at Johannesburg's Wits University (where I majored in archaeology and English), I had become very unfit. I was a typical student: I studied hard enough to pass my subjects each year, I partied, I became involved in student politics and the politics of the time, and I chased the women students as hard as I could, with, I might add, very limited success. Then several factors coalesced at a critical moment to drive me into the inspiring arms of the Comrades Marathon. That first televised race was undoubtedly one factor. At about the same time I played an old boys rugby match at my old school. From early on in the game, I was tired, and by half-time, I was exhausted. The second half of the game seemed interminable, and I remember frequently asking the referee how much time was left until with immense relief, I heard him blow the whistle for full-time. This had never happened to me before. In my school days, I had never grown tired of chasing the ball and chasing the game. The result of the game had been what mattered most, not the duration. We old boys were trounced in that game, and I was one of our weak links. I was given a firm warning about my state of fitness and about how much it had deteriorated.

At university, I befriended a fellow resident, Jean Leger. To me, he had achieved the impossible: He had run the Comrades in a little over seven hours in 1976. One evening after residence dinner, he invited me back to his room and showed me his Comrade's badge and his beautiful gleaming engraved silver medal in its leather jewellery case. (Yes, in those days the Comrades medal was posted to Comrades finishers, fully engraved and with a letter congratulating you and permitting you to order a tie or blazer from a sports shop in Pietermaritzburg.) I was star-struck, and I passionately coveted earning my own engraved Comrades medal, preferably a silver, one just like Jean's.

Months into my training journey for the Comrades, my beautiful girlfriend Elaine broke up with me. This catastrophic event tore a hole in my heart and had a massive impact on my life, both negatively and positively. While for many weeks I was in emotional pain (the first cut is the deepest), I also carried a burning desire to prove myself, and this apparent failure in my life drove me to prove that I could succeed and that I could conquer the toughest of challenges. The Comrades gave me an immense sense of purpose.

While a suppressed libido played a part in my journey to the Comrades, the events of June 1976 were the ultimate catalyst. Though I had started running a few days before the Soweto riots of June 16, my motivation was spurred on by the political turmoil of the time and the powerlessness I felt at being at the mercy of circumstance. The Comrades would give me the chance to wrest back some control of my universe and give myself a challenge of which I could be proud. Now I had an even greater sense of purpose and a burning desire to strive for something positive in a very unhappy universe. When I ventured out to run that first short distance around the Wits rugby fields, there was no other purpose. I was not trying to lose weight, and I was not running for my health. The Ancel Keys US health diet was only to curse the world the following year. In those days, we were all skinny, and we were all partially Banting without knowing it. No, I was running with one goal in mind: Reaching the Comrades Marathon finish line at the end of May 1977. From the very beginning, I kept a diary, and I recorded every run in it as you, the reader, will see.

This was my most important aid. It was almost better than having a personal coach. Besides, there were no Comrades coaches in those days.

In my early training diaries, I often mixed miles and kilometres to measure and record distance. At times I may appear to be confused. My excuse is that all the early textbooks and athletics magazines I read were American or British, and they used Imperial measurements. However, South Africa used the metric system. I hope you, the reader, will forgive me my bilingual approach to miles and kilometres. In those days, we used both.

TRAINING DIARY:

June 1976

to

May 1977

June 1976

> **JUNE 8**: *Ten minutes around Wits rugby fields. Tired at the end. Walked one lap. Pushed myself the last lap. Coughed a bit, wheezed a lot. My fingers are stiff with cold. I can hardly write. I enjoyed my run immensely.*

The journey had begun, and it was not the most auspicious of starts, but the journey must start somewhere for all of us. Initially, I recorded the time I spent running or walking. Later I switched to the distance covered. Amazingly, I wrote this in my diary: *"I must try and make each run a challenge. The essential thing is motivation. I must keep myself interested. I must keep the flame burning. I am going to have to train in a manner I have never trained before. I am going to have to cover long, time-consuming distances and I am going to have to organise my time. The goal for the next few weeks is to get used to running regularly."*

Importantly, I made that first run extremely easy and gentle. By restricting my first run to a few laps of a flat rugby field, I ensured that I would have no problem with running again the next day and for the days and weeks after that. Too many novices run too fast and too far when they start running. As a result, they find running an unpleasant experience. Most would honestly describe running as a chore. "I don't enjoy running. I enjoy having run". As a result, the first half-decent excuse they have not to run (foul weather, work commitments, or lack of motivation) brings their running ambitions to a grinding halt. I did not realise it at the time, but those first running steps were the greatest gift I have ever given myself. Running was to become a vital part of my life, and 44 years later, I still run almost every day and have run well over 200 000 kilometres. Most importantly, I still derive great joy from my running. I sincerely hope that you, the Comrades novice, will also start a lifelong love affair with our sport.

There were three venues that I ran to and from in those early days. One was the College House, Men's Hall of Residence at Wits University. This first run was from my room in residence and around the nearby rugby fields. The second venue was my parent's house in Homestead Avenue, Bryanston, and the third venue was my girlfriend, Elaine's house in Northcliff. During the holidays I ran from my parent's house and during the term from the residence. Most weekends, I was at Elaine's house. I hope you, the reader, will forgive me the confusion. One thing was constant: All three venues were situated in Johannesburg's beneficial high altitude, and hills surrounded all three. I could not have selected a better training environment.

JUNE 9: *Played squash in the morning. Evening run for 15 minutes. Ran at an easier pace than yesterday. The intense cold was hurting my ears and fingers—no coughing or wheezing.*

I recorded all physical activity in my training diary. I still do. In fact, I have always taken note of the complete physical exertion of each day. If some other activity has taken its toll, I will trim my running plans or adjust my schedule. It is interesting that I found it very cold. Our winters are, without a doubt, not as intensely cold as they were in the seventies. At that time, I also ran at night because I was embarrassed to be seen running. Runners were not the common everyday sight they are today. I wrote, *"It has been absolute rubbish that I have not had exercise as part of my life for so long."*

> **JUNE 10**: *Bad run, stomach cramps (ran too soon after eating). Could not maintain a decent pace. Ran three separate sprints afterwards to compensate.*

Learning early on that not every run is fun, and that running, food and tummies often disagree. I have never eaten anything before a race, and I never ate anything or had breakfast before any Comrades Marathon. I am always too nervous to eat, and that awful feeling of a half-eaten banana sitting under my Adam's apple while I am trying to run a major hill is something I can do without. Besides, even the skinniest of fat-adapted athletes understand that we have thousands of calories in the form of body fat waiting to be burned.

> **JUNE 11**: *Played squash in the morning. Short ten-minute run in the evening.*

> **JUNE 12**: *Absolutely exhausted after a game of rugby in the afternoon sun.*

Old boys match at Woodmead, my old school. Running had not yet begun to dominate my life, but it would not be long before it grew in importance. Surprisingly, for a small guy, I was quite a good player. I loved to play scrumhalf, and I was not afraid to tackle. I am still a passionate rugby fan and a brilliant armchair critic. I did not realise it at the time, but this was to be the last game of rugby I ever played.

> JUNE 13: *Woke up very stiff.*
> *Full of aches. Walked five miles.*

WEEKLY MILEAGE:

Approximately 20 kilometres.

> JUNE 14: *Shins very stiff, but otherwise a good run.*

I forgot to write down the distance. As I mentioned at the start of this diary, in those early days, I often only recorded the time I spent running. Some coaches and runners still do this.

> JUNE 15: *Very enjoyable run. Decided to run*
> *around the Wits campus exploring. Finished*
> *with a few laps around the rugby field.*
>
> JUNE 16: *Missed!*

All South Africans know about the awful events of this day, and what can one say about one of the most momentous and terrible days in South Africa's history? News was filtering back to us on the Wits campus that there were mass riots in Soweto and that thousands of students and young school children were protesting against a government Bantu Education decree requiring that they be taught at least half their lessons in Afrikaans. We heard that children had been shot and killed and that the army and the police were almost at war with the demonstrators. I remember smoke on the horizon curling up into the air from the direction of Soweto. All-day long, Wits students were trying to get information and to mobilise to do something in support of the Soweto children. It was a chaotic, adrenalin-filled day. Running training laps around campus or on the Wits rugby fields seemed trivial.

Queen Elizabeth Bridge, Braamfontein, Johannesburg,
where we were marching in sympathy with
the Soweto students until the police broke up
our protest. Here my classmate, Christine, is
bleeding after being assaulted by the police.

JUNE 17: *No run. Depressed, saddened and smarting from a couple of bruises from railway workers' kicks and police truncheons.*

We (students) held a mass meeting on the lawns of the university's library and then we picketed on Jan Smuts Avenue. We then tried to set off on two protest marches across the Queen Elizabeth Bridge and into the Johannesburg CBD. We did not get far. The Queen Elizabeth Bridge crosses the railway lines, and we were set upon by railway workers and the railway security police. They were dressed in leather jackets wielding sticks and sjamboks, planks of wood and chains. That march was quickly scattered and dispersed with several students limping back to campus concussed and bleeding. We regrouped, however, and after Helen Joseph had delivered a passionate and rousing speech, we set off again. This time it was the police's turn to attack us. Leaping from trucks, they encircled us on the same bridge and with batons raised they charged at us. Several of us were kicked, beaten and chased back to campus. Some of our leaders were arrested. In front of me, Christine, a delightful young lady in my archaeology class, was beaten over the head and, bleeding profusely, was then arrested. The savagery was horrific; it was a civil war. South Africans were brutalising and maiming fellow South Africans. I had not known a blacker day.

> **JUNE 18**: *Ran down Jan Smuts Avenue from the University. Pace quite quick on the way out. Struggled on the way back. Disliked the lack of privacy.*

Given the chaos and sadness of the previous two days, I felt that the best way I could restore some order to my life was to run again. Youngsters in Soweto had died, many were fleeing into exile never to return, and some were under arrest in detention. The Minister of Justice, Jimmy Kruger, banned all outside meetings and gatherings. The following year, Kruger was the minister in charge when Steve Biko was killed while in police custody. All I could do was to restore some semblance of order to my life by grasping at my dream to run the Comrades Marathon and by running again.

I was still such a naïve runner and diarist, and I did not bother to record time or distance. I remember the run being roughly six kilometres. I also had not learnt to pace myself and started too quickly. Finally, I was venturing out onto the public roads for the first time. Runners were not a common sight in those days, so I was aware of motorists staring at me, and I felt embarrassed. Women runners were a particularly rare sight, and with my shoulder-length blond hair and slim build, from a distance, I looked like a female runner. The stares from motorists were acutely unnerving. On more than one occasion, motorists stopped to ask if I needed help. The events of June 16 had driven me to accelerate my training. I was not going to successfully complete a Comrades Marathon by running laps of the Wits rugby fields or by exploring the campus. I needed to venture further afield.

JUNE 19: *Freezing day, bundled up against the cold. Kept the pace slow.*

Again, I probably ran about five to six kilometres.

JUNE 20: *Ran at a slower pace for 30 minutes with my great mate, David Dyzenhaus. (David is now Professor of Law and Philosophy at the University of Toronto.) Now I know I can run for an hour.*

I was gradually starting to believe in myself and, like all novice runners, starting to expand my horizons.

WEEKLY MILEAGE:
Approximately 30 kilometres.

Sharing a bath with my great mate and Comrades second David Dyzenhaus, the future Toronto University Professor of Law and Philosophy. This photo was taken a couple of years earlier when we were on what is now known as "matric rage". We were in Plettenberg Bay and the seaside town was experiencing water shortages. Residents were asked to save water!

JUNE 21: *No run. University residence dance the night before.*

I was undoubtedly tired and possibly hungover. Running was still not a major priority in my life.

JUNE 22: *Started too quickly and struggled on my run back. Ran with David again.*

Once again, probably about five to six kilometres. Early on, I was learning that starting too quickly can be disastrous.

My favourite strategy of starting cautiously was gradually being created.

> JUNE 23: *Twenty-minute run.*
>
> JUNE 24: *Ran for 32 minutes.*
>
> JUNE 25: *Forty-minute run. Amazing.*
> *No problems with distance.*
>
> JUNE 26: *Ran a loop around the Bryanston Country*
> *Club (almost 7 km). The cars are annoying.*

Learning early on that cars and runners don't go well together. It is also worth remembering that in those days, runners were a relatively uncommon sight on the roads. Nowadays we don't give them a second glance, but in the 1970s, runners were a rare species.

> JUNE 27: *Rest day.*

WEEKLY MILEAGE:
Approximately 35 kilometres.

> JUNE 28: *Favourite route in 31 minutes. Arches and*
> *ankles sore. Next goal: Break 30 minutes for the route.*

Slight niggles as my body adapt to the running load and interesting that even in these early days, I was already setting goals and targets for myself.

> **JUNE 29**: *Favourite route, but sore feet to begin with.*

As our bodies adapt to the workload, we can experience quite a few aches and niggles. As they embark on a training programme, all runners must exercise caution and be wary of injuries. They need to listen to their bodies.

> **JUNE 30**: *Eight-kilometre or so fast running.*
> *Finished running very quickly.*

Clearly, I did not listen to my body in those days. During that first month, I ran 85 kilometres, and at the end of the month, I knew had begun the journey to the Comrades. Most importantly, I had taken my first running steps, and I had committed to train for the marathon. There were distractions, but I had kept going and this at the coldest and darkest time of year.

July 1976

JULY 1: *Laps of Zoo Lake Park for 30 minutes. Felt a bit stiff.*

JULY 2: *Laps of Zoo Lake Park again. Legs still stiff.*

JULY 3: *No run – recovery day with a force-10 hangover.*

It is difficult to explain to a younger generation the enormous impact that the hilarious, insane lunatics known as Monty Python had on us and in particular me, in those days, but suffice it to say I was, and still am, a die-hard fan. Cleese, Chapman, Jones, Idle, Gilliam, and Palin were as important to me as were Lennon, McCartney, Harrison and Starkey. What the Beatles were to music, the Pythons were to comedy and satire. In the same way that I can sing the lyrics of any Beatles song, I can also quote huge chunks of the Pythons' *And Now For Something Completely Different* or *Life of Brian.* Sometimes when I'm training, I might hum parts of *Abbey Road* or the *Double White* album to myself. At other times I will quickly mutter a Python quote to mates or myself when the running is getting tough. "Cheer up, Brian. See, it's not so bad up here once you get used to it", or I might whistle the famous Python song, "Always Look on the Bright Side of Life". On the evening before this missed run, a group of Wits Python fans held a charity comedy evening where they showed the two Monty Python films that had been released at that stage, along with a host of BBC Python sketches. They also served cheap wine in great plastic barrels. I was never going to make a run that morning.

> JULY 4: *Eighteen-kilometre run with*
> *Roly Whittaker. Furthest I have run. We ran*
> *very slowly. L.S.D. – 1 hour, 55 minutes.*

A new distance barrier had been broken for me while running with my stepfather that morning. I had never run that far. Roly, a doctor, had been running for a couple of years by then. He was a huge early influence in my running life. He had read everything there was to read on running and was an expert on running injuries, training, and nutrition. He was an enthusiastic fan of George Sheehan, an American cardiologist, runner, and writer who wrote for *Runner's World* magazine and whose book, *Running and Being: The Total experience,* was a bestseller. It could be argued that Roly was my first coach. He was the first to say to me that I could be a very good Comrades runner. Sadly, he was never fast enough to qualify for the Comrades himself, but I know it gave him great pleasure to watch my progress in the race. I owe him so much.

Divorce is never pleasant for family members, but in Roly, I gained a second wise and loving father. The "L.S.D." I refer to in this case is not a hallucinogenic drug but stands for "Long Slow Distance" and was a popular training method in the seventies. Tim Noakes believes the first exponent of this method of training was Arthur Newton, the father of modern distance running. Certainly, the concept of running slowly but covering more distance was popularised by Joe Henderson, the first editor-in-chief of *Runner's World* magazine and a renowned coach. My running improved immensely once I started running regular long, slow runs with Roly on the weekends and later with my Wits teammates. To this day, I still believe that long training runs for the Comrades Marathon should be run in the L.S.D.-style, i.e. slowly and steadily.

> **WEEKLY MILEAGE:**
> **Approximately 50 kilometres.**

> JULY 5: *Zoo Lake run of 30 minutes. Legs stiff, but ran feeling inspired by the approaching Olympic Games.*

Even though the sports boycott against apartheid South Africa meant South Africa would not participate in the 1976 Olympic Games, I was still inspired by the athletes who were going to participate. I was keen to see the great distance track clashes of Lasse Viren and Brendan Foster at 5 000/10 000 metres, John Walker and Filbert Bayi over 1 500 metres, and of course the men's marathon. (1 500 metres were the longest distance women were permitted to run in the Olympics in the seventies.) Many of my runs in those days were fuelled by fantasies of winning the gold medal in the Olympic Games Marathon, or as ridiculous as it seemed, winning the Comrades Marathon.

> **JULY 6**: *Half an hour run. Legs stiff and sore from the 18 kilometres I ran two days ago.*

> **JULY 7**: *Thirty-five-minute run. Stepping up the time on the road wearing new Tiger Montreal's.*

I was doing the correct thing – slowly increasing my training distances. Tiger Montreal running shoes were considered state-of-the-art in those days. Onitsuka Tiger later became the Asics shoes we know today.

Lasse Viren with his Tiger Montreal's in 1976. (Associated Press.) Many athletics fans consider Lasse Viren's racing streak in July 1976 to have been some of the greatest quality days of racing ever witnessed. In those few days from July 23 to July 31, Viren raced the 10 000 metres heats and final. He then ran the 5 000 metres heats, semi-final and final. He won the gold medal in both these events, completing a "double-double". (He had won the same two events at the Munich Olympics four years earlier.) For good measure, he entered the marathon the afternoon after his 5 000 metres triumph. He finished 5th in 02:13. In all, Viren racked up about 70 kilometres of intense racing in that short time.

> JULY 8: *A shorter run of 20 minutes.*
> *University work priorities.*
>
> JULY 9: *No run. University work.*
>
> JULY 10: *Twelve kilometres in 01:05.*

I am starting to measure my distances in kilometres or miles and time.

> JULY 11: *Forty-six-minute run – about ten kilometres.*

WEEKLY MILEAGE:
Approximately 45 kilometres.

> JULY 12: *Ran from university residence to*
> *Parkwood shops and back in 39 minutes.*

Eager to measure my improvement, I timed myself. From time to time this is acceptable, but many novices don't understand that they can't expect to get faster every time they run and that they can put too much pressure on themselves to improve constantly.

> JULY 13: *Forty-five-minute run to Judith Road and*
> *back. Did not enjoy the run. Tight right knee.*
>
> JULY 14: *Judith Road and back in 29:45.*

I am continuing to time myself!

> **JULY 15**: *Amazing run. Felt incredible. Running into a strong wind up Jan Smuts Avenue and still my fastest run to Parkwood shops and back to university residence in 38 minutes.*

I was still pushing myself too hard on each run. I needed to learn that not every run has to break a personal best (p.b.). However, this was an early sign that I would develop into a strong uphill runner.

> **JULY 16**: *No run. Day off.*

> **JULY 17**: *Ran from home in Bryanston to Elaine's house in Northcliff in 47 minutes. Tough slog through Randburg.*

Amazing what youthful libido can do for a young runner!

> **JULY 18**: *Midday run from Elaine's house back to university residence in just over 40 minutes. Sun made me feel faint.*

Midday in the African sun, even in winter, can be tough.

WEEKLY MILEAGE:
Approximately 50 kilometres.

> JULY 19: *Ran from my residence to Judith Road,*
> *Emmarentia, and back in just under 45 minutes.*
> *Slowly on the way out, very fast on the way in.*

An early sign of my favourite racing tactic in later years.
Start slowly and then pick up the pace. Finish very strongly.

WEEKLY MILEAGE:

Just over 50 kilometres or so.

> JULY 20: *Parkwood shops and back in*
> *37:45. Getting faster with each run.*

The problem once again is that I was putting pressure on
myself to get faster every time I ran. I was going to be disappointed if the next run wasn't quicker still. Eventually,
for a variety of reasons, it just can't be faster.

> JULY 21: *Longer run from residence to*
> *Rosebank and back in 48 minutes.*

As discussed in the introduction to this book, Jean Leger,
a fellow resident and silver medallist (07:09:00), invited
me to his room where he gave me invaluable advice and
training tips. He helped to fuel the Comrades fire further.
He also advised me to run on my own for the rest of the
year to build a fitness foundation and then to join the
university's marathon club in the new year.

JULY 22: *Time restraints. One short 30-minute run.*

The beauty of running, unlike so many other sports, is that its simplicity allows us to squeeze short, quick runs in when time is limited.

JULY 23: *Longer one-hour run from home in Bryanston. Tough slog up Peter Place.*

JULY 24: *No run.*

JULY 25: *A charity walk of 11 kilometres in the morning. Managed a 6.8-kilometre run around Bryanston Country Club in 26:30.*

WEEKLY MILEAGE:
Approximately 50 kilometres.

JULY 26: *Reverse route around Bryanston Country Club (6.8 km) in 26:15.*

The Montreal Olympic Games 10 000-metre final, inspired by my heroes Viren, Lopes, and Foster. It was a sensational race, and I remember being astonished that human beings could run ten kilometres in under twenty-eight minutes. Years later, I was to meet some of my heroes.

Many years later, with my hero, Carlos Lopes.
(Olympic 10 000 m medallist 1976. Olympic
Marathon champion of 1984 and three times
World Cross-country champion.) He asked me
to send Zola Budd his best wishes – they were
both World Cross-country champions in 1985.

JULY 27: *New route from home into Randburg
(7 km). Fast pace. Lower shins very sore.*

The first sign that my personal biomechanics would often
determine my later injuries. I am a heavy pronator (in 1976,
I would not have understood what "pronator" meant), and
my over-pronation would often lead to soleus and calf
muscle tears. In those early days, I diagnosed these injuries
as "sore shins". Later I would understand that I needed to
train in heavier supportive shoes and only use light racing
shoes for races. One of the greatest discoveries any runner
can make is to learn his or her own biomechanical pecu-
liarities. Enormous amounts of frustration can be avoided.
However, the process takes time and experience, and many

Comrades novices experience so much frustration and anguish as injuries threaten to destroy their dreams. Just because the Comrades champion wears a certain brand and model of shoe does not mean that this shoe will work for every runner. It is worth visiting a specialist running shoe shop, possibly paying a little bit more, but receiving expert advice rather than choosing your own shoes in a giant chain store.

> JULY 28: *Raced myself again on the July 26-route (6.8 km). Really pushed hard, and in the midday sun. Very, very tired coming up Homestead Avenue. New best time of 25:42.*
>
> JULY 29: *Randburg route again (7 km). Shins not too sore. Heat and a headwind but ran the route in 25 minutes.*
>
> JULY 30: *Randburg route again (7 km). Shins behaved.*
>
> JULY 31: *New route. Ran for 28 minutes. Felt good.*

At the end of the second month, I had run 178 kilometres. So, at the end of my first full month of training, I was starting to build a training foundation. I was a long way from being fit and strong enough to run the Comrades, but I had made a good start and was running consistently. Consistency is one of the keys to successful racing. I had also started running some longer, but slow training runs.

August 1976

> **AUGUST 1**: *Eighteen kilometres with Roly,*
> *my stepfather, at his slower pace – 1 hour, 49 minutes.*
> *Sore legs at the end. (Inspired as Lasse Viren wins*
> *10 000/5 000 metres double at the Montreal Olympics.)*

WEEKLY MILEAGE:
Approximately 60 kilometres.

> **AUGUST 2**: *Bad cold or flu. Ran four kilometres gently.*

We all know it's foolish and worse, potentially dangerous to run when you have the flu, but I'm not sure I was aware of that back in the 1970s. I'm not certain that any of us were.

> **AUGUST 3**: *Flu too bad. No run.*

I think it was the illness that won and forced me to take a break rather than me being sensible.

> **AUGUST 4**: *Another easier run. Just four kilometres.*

> **AUGUST 5**: *Felt faint and nauseous after my run. Eight kilometres around Brescia House School from home in 38 minutes. Horrible run but I forced myself to keep going.*

Foolish and dangerous. But like so many runners, I was and still am stubborn when it comes to my running.

> **AUGUST 6**: *Long 11-kilometre walk to Elaine's house. Coughed a bit.*

Slightly more sensible.

> **AUGUST 7**: *A 35-minute run around Northcliff, including steep Northcliff Hill. Still not feeling great.*

> **AUGUST 8**: *Ran home from Northcliff – 11 kilometres in 46 minutes. Ran too fast in the midday sun. Very tired and thirsty at the end. Must learn to slow down.*

Like so many new runners, and deeply infected with "desperately-keen-titis", I was still pushing every run too hard and too fast. Wisely, I had started to notice the problem and was trying to do something about it.

WEEKLY MILEAGE:
Approximately 50 kilometres.

> **AUGUST 9**: *Managed to "slow down". Brescia House*
> *(10 km). Tried to force myself to slow down but*
> *still two minutes faster than the last occasion I ran*
> *this route. Ran very strongly up Bryanston Drive.*
> *Could have knocked more time off if I had raced.*

I was getting fitter with each outing. Many new runners give up because they perceive that they are not making any progress and are not getting fitter. Quite often, they simply haven't given themselves enough time. I believe the results start to show, and running starts to become an addiction after at least three months of commitment.

> **AUGUST 10**: *Rest day. No run*

> **AUGUST 11**: *Ten-kilometre run from Bryanston*
> *home to the bridge near Fourways in 41 minutes.*

I was running four minutes per kilometre in training – as a novice runner!

> **AUGUST 12**: *Very cold wind. Same route*
> *as yesterday in 39 minutes.*

Still racing myself and now under four minutes per kilometre!

> **AUGUST 13**: *Time problems.*
> *Four-kilometre run in 16 minutes.*

> **AUGUST 14**: *Seven-kilometre charity walk.*

> **AUGUST 15:** *Bryanston Golf Course route – ten kilometres in 45 minutes.*

> **WEEKLY MILEAGE:**
> **Approximately 50 kilometres.**

> **AUGUST 16:** *End of holidays, back to residence at Wits University. July 12-route (9 km) from university residence to Parkwood shops and back in 36:40. Big improvement.*

The training was paying off. Longer runs and regular running were producing results.

> **AUGUST 17:** *Well, I proved that yesterday's performance was not a fluke. Nearly four minutes faster on my residence to Judith Road and back in 41 minutes. Turned in just over 20 minutes. That is enough of the testing. Take it easy in future.*
> Further proof that I was getting fitter.

> **AUGUST 18:** *Sore right knee. Missed run.*

Two hard runs in a row had some consequences. Wisely I knew I should rest.

> **AUGUST 19:** *Forty-five minutes in the heat of the day. Felt sluggish.*

AUGUST 20: *Ran from Elaine's house in Northcliff to Wits residence in 45 minutes. Baking hot so kept it easy.*

AUGUST 21: *No run.*

AUGUST 22: *Ran from Elaine's house to parents' house in Bryanston in 49 minutes. Also played tennis, so quite tired.*

At this early stage, I was recording all physical effort and taking this into account. As I mentioned earlier in this book, too many runners forget to acknowledge all their physical efforts in a full day's activities. To this day, I continue to record any hard, physical exertion as part of a training day.

WEEKLY MILEAGE:

Approximately 45 kilometres.

AUGUST 23: *Very late night and little sleep so one easy six-kilometre run.*

AUGUST 24: *Men's residence to Rosebank shops and back. Kept the pace easy – 49 minutes of running.*

AUGUST 25: *Hot and dry midday run. Felt drained. Stopped after five kilometres.*

Sometimes, it is wise to realise that your run is not working and to call it a day. I believe it was Joe Henderson, editor-in-chief of *Runner's World* magazine, who used what he called the ten-minute test to aid his running. If he was having a bad run, he would continue running for ten minutes. If he still felt awful, he would return home. If things improved, as they often do, he would continue running.

> **AUGUST 26**: *Ran July 12-route (nine kilometres from university residence to Parkwood shops and back), but ran without a tracksuit top for the first time. Nearly three minutes faster with a time of 36:35.*

I was starting to learn that "less is more" when it comes to running in the cold. Too many runners are too bundled up and insulated from the cold when they run in winter. The working human body generates tremendous warmth, and after a few hundred metres, I always regret over-dressing. As long as my ears and fingers are covered, I am happy even on a very cold day. I prefer running in light clothing, even on the coldest of days. Many years later (1987 and 1995), I was reminded that less is more when I ran the Nanisivik Midnight Sun Ultra 84-kilometre Marathon on Baffin Island, Canada, 800 kilometres inside the Arctic Circle. I started those races heavily bundled up against the cold Arctic air but finished both races wearing only leggings, gloves and a light T-shirt.

> **AUGUST 27**: *Ran the July 27-route of seven kilometres in 28:35 (from home into Randburg and back). Quite tired.*
>
> **AUGUST 28**: *No run.*

> **AUGUST 29**: *Twenty-kilometre very slow run with my stepfather, Roly. Legs were stiff and sore at the end, but I still had plenty of running left in me.*

WEEKLY MILEAGE:

Approximately 50 kilometres.

> **AUGUST 30**: *No run because of work pressure. Irritated about having to miss the run.*

After all, I had to complete my university degree!

> **AUGUST 31**: *A six-kilometre run in 25:30.*

Despite some health setbacks, I had continued to run consistently and during my third month of training ran 200 kilometres.

September 1976

SEPTEMBER 1: *Slow eight-kilometre run.*

SEPTEMBER 2: *Ran the August 23-route (an easy 6 km) in 26:10. Very pleased.*

SEPTEMBER 3: *No run.*

SEPTEMBER 4: *Ran from Elaine's house in Northcliff to my Wits residence at midday – baking hot outside. Despite the heat, it felt easy, and I was surprised at my relatively fast time of 40:10.*

SEPTEMBER 5: *Annoyed but unable to run due to work pressure.*

I was starting to get irritated if something interfered with a run. Clearly, I was addicted, and I had a goal in mind.

WEEKLY MILEAGE:
Approximately 40 kilometres.

> **SEPTEMBER 6**: *Another slow 20-kilometre run*
> *with Roly. A bit stiff at the end. A vicious German*
> *Shepherd attacked us. We stood our ground, and*
> *it backed off, but it was a scary moment.*

Every runner will eventually be confronted by an angry dog. I have found that the best thing to do is to stop running and turn and face the dog. Trying to run away is hopeless. Dogs pursue running figures, and they are much faster than us. It can help to bend to pick up a rock or stick, or even an imaginary rock or stick. Often vicious dogs are serial offenders, and they have had many rocks thrown at them and from experience they back away.

> **SEPTEMBER 7**: *Rosebank route from*
> *my residence in 46:10. Felt great.*
>
> **SEPTEMBER 8**: *Rosebank run again. Wondered*
> *why it felt tough, and I was breathing hard. Had*
> *a tough climb up Jan Smuts Avenue. Discovered*
> *why I had struggled when I noticed my time*
> *at the finish: 44:25! Almost two minutes faster*
> *than I have run before. Starting to get fitter.*

Years later, while running up Polly Shortts in the 1988 Comrades, I began to worry as I felt I was struggling while climbing the famous hill. Only after the race, I discovered why I thought I had been struggling: I had run up the 1.8-kilometre hill in under eight minutes!

> SEPTEMBER 9: *Tired and sore legs after three hard days of running. Ran my Rosebank route in 45:35. Pushed the last two kilometres. I am developing hard blisters at the tips of my toes.*

I was soon to learn that runner's feet and toes are not the prettiest sights in the world of sport.

> SEPTEMBER 10: *Rest day.*

> SEPTEMBER 11: *Ran to Elaine's house from Wits University. Very hot. The last climb was tough – 37:50.*

> SEPTEMBER 12: *Social tennis all day. Short run in the evening.*

WEEKLY MILEAGE:

Approximately 50 kilometres.

> SEPTEMBER 13: *Rosebank route. Felt very demotivated but ran well on the return leg – 45:10.*

> SEPTEMBER 14: *Rosebank route plus a little extra (10 – 11 km). Ran too soon after eating. Felt full, slow, awkward, heavy and bloated.*

As mentioned elsewhere in this book, I learnt that I cannot have any food in my stomach when I run. To this day, I run every race on an empty stomach. I ate nothing before the start of every Comrades Marathon I ever ran. Some runners feel that they must eat something. I was the opposite, and I still am.

> **SEPTEMBER 15**: *Rest day.*

> **SEPTEMBER 16**: *Very fast six-kilometre run. Forgot to time myself, but it felt fast.*

> **SEPTEMBER 17**: *Rest day.*

I attended passionate meetings on campus to vote in favour of opening Wits University to students of all races. It was decided to hold a referendum in order to measure the support for this. Unsurprisingly, this motion was supported, which was in direct opposition to the government's policy at the time. (Not often, but sometimes, there are indeed matters that are more important than running!)

> **SEPTEMBER 18**: *Eight kilometres around Bryanston. A lot of hills and hot. Had to push hard up the hills.*

> **SEPTEMBER 19**: *Enjoyable Rosebank run in 46:20. Did not have to push the pace.*

WEEKLY MILEAGE:
Approximately 50 kilometres.

> **SEPTEMBER 20**: *Swotting for exams, so I am pushed for time. Just a fast five-kilometre run.*

The running was a welcome break from hours of swotting. At times, our priorities change, and exams meant restricted running time. I decided I would try and run at least five kilometres each day. Little did I know then that 35 years later, I would start a love affair with the five-kilometre distance in the form of parkrun. As I write, parkrun is the single most important running event in my life at the moment.

(Note: For more information on parkrun, please see the glossary at the end of this book.)

> **SEPTEMBER 21**: *Rosebank run. Cooler evening. Decided to run harder and turned back in a fast time to record 42:15 for the route.*

Early on in my running career, I was comfortable with running both in the evenings and in the mornings. In later years, in pursuit of faster Comrades times, I would run twice a day – mornings and evenings – almost every day.

(Note: For the reader who is interested in how I trained in later years in order to win the Comrades Marathon, please go to my website www.brucefordyce.com. Here you will find my e-books where I discuss my training for the 1986 and 1988 Comrades Marathons.)

> **SEPTEMBER 22**: *Decided to run a fast "end of Judith Road and back"-route. Turned in 20 minutes again (August 17) and then held the pace. I felt good. Slight headwind blowing. Broke 40 minutes (39:25) for a run that used to take me over 45 minutes.*

The value of having a training diary is beautifully illustrated here. I could compare times and monitor my progress.

> SEPTEMBER 23: *Exam time problems. Just one fast five-kilometre run. Ran as hard as I could.*

Three-day closure of Wits in support of the demand to admit black students to the university. I remember it as a time of anger and passionate debate. There were meetings and speeches from distinguished guests in the Great Hall. Our Vice-Chancellor, Professor "Boz" Bozolli, spoke in favour of the demand, and John Kane-Berman (ex S.R.C.-president) gave a stirring speech as did Chief Mangosuthu Buthelezi (Zulu tribal leader and politician). Percy Qoboza, the editor of *The World* newspaper, was given a standing ovation after he challenged white South Africans to demand the end of apartheid. In the afternoons, we were making posters, discussing the latest developments, strategising, and getting together to eat Wits "slap" chips and gravy while drinking beer and cheap red wine. In all the excitement, passionate demonstrations, and stirring chaos, it was impossible to find time to run.

WEEKLY MILEAGE:
Approximately 30 kilometres.

> SEPTEMBER 27: *Cross with myself for having*
> *a three-day layoff from training. "That's bad".*
> *I went back to training, determined to run a*
> *cracker. Judith Road and back (July 14-route).*
> *Smashed that antiquated time in 27:50!*

I was getting fitter and faster, but I was also learning by default that resting helps to create strong, fast legs.

> SEPTEMBER 28: *Ran eight kilometres. It was a cold*
> *night so ran in a tracksuit top—about 35 minutes.*

As discussed earlier, wearing a tracksuit top is something I would no longer do, no matter how cold it was.

> SEPTEMBER 29: *Ran August 16/July 12-route again*
> *in 37:45. Something felt wrong. Felt weighed down and*
> *heavy. I was very tired after running up the hills.*

Once again failing to understand that you cannot improve every single time!

> SEPTEMBER 30: *A very fast six-kilometre run*
> *while fighting a strong headwind. Must try and*
> *find the time for more mileage this next month.*

I was beginning to realise that to improve, I had to run much more and for longer distances.

At the end of the fourth month, I had run 165 kilometres. In future years, I would run 165 kilometres (100 miles) in one week, but in only my fourth month of training, I was getting fitter and better.

October 1976

OCTOBER 1: *I was pushed for time, so did a slow five-kilometre run.*

OCTOBER 2: *Missed – no run.*

OCTOBER 3: *I think I have the flu. Felt cold and sore before I ran. I went out intending to run a slow six kilometres but after four kilometres developed a painful stitch in the pit of my stomach. I stopped for a few seconds and then ran another kilometre. Stitch returned, so I stopped again. In the end, I covered six kilometres, but I could feel the flu draining me.*

As I discussed earlier in this book, in the 1970s, we were not that knowledgeable about the dangers of exercising with flu-like symptoms, but we now have no excuse. What I did that day was extremely dangerous. Rest is the only sensible response to catching flu.

> **WEEKLY MILEAGE:**
> **Approximately 35 kilometres.**

> **OCTOBER 7:** *I have been sick with tonsillitis, so I decided to rest and restart my running with an easy jog and then build it up again. I ran for ten minutes around the rugby fields and then five minutes of faster running.*

The sensible decision was to miss a few days while my body fought off the flu I had caught.

> **OCTOBER 8:** *Another shorter, easier run around Wits Campus – about four kilometres.*
>
> **OCTOBER 9:** *Another day off.*
>
> **OCTOBER 10:** *Ran five kilometres from Elaine's house in Northcliff to Westpark Cemetery and back. Much better. Beautiful sunset.*

I am starting to enjoy the other gifts of running that are not just about getting fitter and faster.

> **WEEKLY MILEAGE:**
> **Approximately 15 – 20 kilometres.**

> **OCTOBER 11:** *Ran the September 29-route again. Slight stomach cramps at the end.*

> **OCTOBER 12:** *Despite a sore throat and turning my ankle, ran my Rosebank route from Men's Residence and back. New p.b. of 41:25.*

Despite the sore throat and twisted ankle, I felt good and decided to go for it.

> **OCTOBER 13:** *Ran seven kilometres. Nearly died! I had difficulty breathing through my sore throat, and my limbs were sore and stiff for the first five kilometres. That run did me no good.*

I was correct; the run was a stupid idea. My comment, "I nearly died" could have come true. In the first few years of my running career, I often suffered from colds, flu and tonsillitis. In 1980, I had my tonsils removed, and my running really took off. I experienced fewer days lost to illness, and I just felt generally fitter and stronger. In 1981, I won my first Comrades Marathon.

> **OCTOBER 14:** *After last night's debacle I decided to try and run two shorter runs, three hours apart. Ran an easy four-kilometre run and then a five-kilometre.*

Compounding the stupidity of the previous evening! I do not know what I was thinking. I do know I was not thinking wisely.

OCTOBER 15: *Feeling a lot better and ran seven kilometres. I am now ready for longer runs.*

OCTOBER 16: *Exam commitments. No run.*

OCTOBER 17: *Exam commitments. No run.*

WEEKLY MILEAGE:
Approximately 45 kilometres.

OCTOBER 18: *Rosebank run – nine kilometres. Cold night – 43:00.*

OCTOBER 19: *Well, that was the oddest run I have ever attempted. Had run about a kilometre of my Rosebank route when I met a damsel in distress with a broken-down motorbike. Ended up helping her to push her bike for miles to a garage. Had no time to finish my planned run, so dashed two kilometres back.*

OCTOBER 20: *Very bloated feeling. Too soon after supper. Lethargic Rosebank route. When I smelt home, I pushed it.*

I can't believe I ate supper before running, but as a student in residence, I suppose I had to eat at the prescribed times or starve! Now I would never eat a main meal before running.

My right shin is very sore. Can't decide why.

As I mentioned in July of this book, although I was un-aware of it at the time, I was experiencing another brush with my personal biomechanics. I am a heavy pronator on both feet. In those days, I would not have known what pronation meant. My excessive pronation means I often experience small but painful muscle tears of the calf and soleus muscles. It was not until 1982 that the great Tim Noakes diagnosed my problem. Tim was in transit at the old Jan Smuts Airport (O.R. Tambo), and I dashed to the airport so that he could look at my running biomechanics. I jogged up and down the airport departure lounge, and Tim advised me to wear supportive, anti-pronation shoes when training and to only wear light racing shoes when racing. Following that vital airport "consultation", I was very rarely troubled again by my excessive pronation. Unfortunately, I hadn't yet met Tim in 1976, so I was to experience a lot of frustration in those early days. Our running styles are all different, and one of the greatest learning experiences for all runners is to understand their own running biomechanics.

> **OCTOBER 21**: *Shin still sore. Ran a new route (8 km) in 33 minutes or so. Then ran one more kilometre.*

Unfortunately, I can now no longer remember exactly what this new route was as I was to run it frequently, but it was probably about seven kilometres.

> **OCTOBER 22**: *Ran seven kilometres in rush hour traffic. Horrible. Wore lighter shoes but shin painful.*

I still hadn't learnt that I needed supportive, heavier shoes.

OCTOBER 23: *No run.*

OCTOBER 24: *Ran 11 kilometres from Elaine's house. Legs still sore.*

> **WEEKLY MILEAGE:**
> **Approximately 50 kilometres.**

OCTOBER 25: *A seven-kilometre run. Took it slowly. Legs/shins more painful in lighter shoes.*

I hope you can sense my frustration at the time.

OCTOBER 26: *Ran the October 21-route. Distance closer to seven kilometres. Right shin really aching now when I run. Wore my new Tiger Montreal's but they can't be the reason for the ache in my shins. If anything, slightly better. Could feel weight and stiffness of the shoes.*

For the benefit of younger runners, the Tiger Montreal (full name Onitsuka Tiger Montreal) was state-of-the-art in 1976 and was named after the Montreal Olympics where Finland's Lasse Viren won the 5 000/10 000 metres double wearing Montreal's with spikes. In later years, Onitsuka Tiger became Asics, a modern brand that everyone knows. The Tiger's stripes are still on the side of the shoe.

In my logbook, I continued to complain about my injury: *This pain is ridiculous. Finished in 29:50.* The frustration of every injured runner surfaces in my comment, "This is ridiculous".

> **OCTOBER 27**: *No time to run. Swotting.*
>
> **OCTOBER 28**: *Ran to Elaine's house. Beautiful run. Pushed the pace the whole way and sprinted the last 0.5 kilometres. Smashed my best time of September 11-run – 34:45.*
>
> **OCTOBER 29**: *Ran back to the university residence from Northcliff. Hot, blustery morning, and rush hour traffic – exhaust fumes were irritating. Ran easily for 43 minutes.*
>
> **OCTOBER 30**: *Swotting. No run.*
>
> **OCTOBER 31**: *Ran October 21-route (8 km). Leg a little better. Motorists hooted encouragement, and some road workers cheered me on—same finishing time as before – 29:50.*

At the end of the fifth month, I had run 154 kilometres. Studying and exams interfered a little with my training, but I was still running fairly consistently, and the dream was in no danger of fading.

WEEKLY MILEAGE:
Approximately 45 kilometres.

November 1976

NOVEMBER 1: *Ran the October 21-route (8 km). Cold night. Raced along. New shoes still a bit stiff but seem to be helping right shin. Very fast – 27:45.*

The new supportive shoes were helping my injury to recover.

NOVEMBER 2: *Ran the October 21-route (8 km) again, this time in reverse. Cold night. Right calf muscle hurting – 29:25.*

Variation helps keep boredom at bay!

NOVEMBER 3: *October 21-route again (8 km). Legs a little better, just the odd twinge. Cold and windy night but apart from wind, ideal running conditions. New p.b. of 27:10.*

NOVEMBER 4: *October 21-route again (8 km) but cold and wet night. Crushed last night's time – 26:25. I think I could run 25 minutes on this course, but not yet.*

NOVEMBER 7: *Missed two days. Made up for them by waking at 05:30 to join my stepfather, Roly, for a 23-kilometre run (measured by car). We ran slow but the morning became very hot.*

Exams. I am proud to say I passed all my subjects in my second year at Wits University that year.

WEEKLY MILEAGE:

Approximately 50 kilometres.

NOVEMBER 8: *October 21-route again (8 km). Shook off exam cobwebs. Forgot to time the run but probably about 28 minutes.*

NOVEMBER 9: *Ran the November 2-route (8 km). Right Achilles giving me trouble but great run. The reverse route is slightly tougher.*

NOVEMBER 10: *Ran the October 21-route again (8 km). Made a concerted effort to break my best time and did it by five seconds – 26:20. Twenty-five minutes is possible, but it would be difficult. Right leg ached from halfway.*

NOVEMBER 11: *Swotting for the exam. Only time for a short four-kilometre run.*

November 12: Pouring with rain. No run.

In later years, rain was not going to stop me. However, lightning is another matter.

> **NOVEMBER 13**: *Fast run to Elaine's house. Left at 18:00. Still very hot and I struggled on hills. Reduced to a crawl on the last hill but recovered at the top and turned up the pace. Reduced October 28 time to 34:30.*

> **NOVEMBER 14**: *What a tough run from Elaine's house back to university residence! Fighting off effects of a late-night party and a hangover. Had to stop a couple of times – 44 minutes!*

Partying and reduced sleep are the enemies of good running.

WEEKLY MILEAGE:
Approximately 45 kilometres.

> **NOVEMBER 15**: *October 21-route (8 km). Took it slow, enjoying the run – 28:20. Right leg annoying.*

> **NOVEMBER 16**: *Exam pressure. Had to miss my run.*

> **NOVEMBER 17**: *October 21-route (8 km). Was going well but then two dogs attacked me. Almost took a chunk out of my hand. Shouted at dogs and faced them and they slunk off. As a result, I was unable to break my best time of 26:30.*

> **NOVEMBER 18**: *Swotting for my last exam. Only time for a quick five-kilometre run. Needed to run. I was restless and couldn't sleep properly two nights ago when I missed my run.*

> **NOVEMBER 21**: *Missed two days for final exams. Ran around Plovers Lake farm. Really hot and conditions gruelling. Only managed about five kilometres.*

Game farm of my friend Mark Read. It is close to the hominid fossil-bearing sites of Kromdraai and Sterkfontein and has a deep cave with its own fossil-bearing breccia.

Plovers Lake is a lovely place to run. I passed small herds of zebra, wildebeest, and impala. I was careful to steer clear of the 1 000-kilogram big eland bull.

> **WEEKLY MILEAGE:**
> **Approximately 20 kilometres.**

> **NOVEMBER 22**: *Clearing alien trees at Plovers Lake farm. Hard work all day. No run.*

Mark's father, Everard Read, paid us a few rand each day to chop down alien trees on his farm. The work was exhausting. I had no energy left for running.

> NOVEMBER 23: *I thought I was running slowly and I thought it was a cool day. I wasn't, and it wasn't. I ran my 6.8 km-Bryanston Country Club route (July 25 time was 26:30). Today I turned in an unbelievable 23:20. I was so amazed that I checked my watch about four times.*

> NOVEMBER 24: *Seven-kilometre route around Bryanston (July 27-route). Terribly, terribly hot. Improved time – 24:25. Am pouring sweat now. No trouble from legs, particularly right leg. It is time I did some racing.*

My competitive juices were starting to flow, and my marked improvement was making me keen to test myself, but it was not until the new year and after becoming a member of the Wits Marathon Club that I would run my first official race.

> NOVEMBER 25: *Had very little time. Ran five kilometres at a reasonable pace.*

> NOVEMBER 26: *Walked five kilometres in the morning and jogged a slow six kilometres in the evening.*

> NOVEMBER 27: *Ran 11 kilometres to Elaine's house. It really is a killer of a run—a slow and gradual climb up to Northcliff Hill. Beat my time from July 17 by a few seconds – 47:25. However, I was held up by two sets of traffic lights.*

A few years later, I would run my first Pirates Half-marathon, which summits Northcliff Hill. Since then, I

have run it several times. It must be the toughest half-marathon in SA.

> **NOVEMBER 28**: *Ran a quick four
> kilometres around Bryanston.*

WEEKLY MILEAGE:
Approximately 50 kilometres.

> **NOVEMBER 29**: *Kept awake at night by an ache
> in my right calf. Ran a ten-minute sprint around
> Homestead Avenue and surrounding streets in
> Bryanston. No calf troubles while running.*
>
> **NOVEMBER 30**: *Rested my leg. No run.*

I ran 168 kilometres in the sixth month since I started
training. As the end of the year was approaching, I was
running about 150 – 200 kilometres a month, and running
had become a part of my life.

December 1976

DECEMBER 1: *Ran July 27-route (7 km) to start the new month off. I need a couple more seven-kilometre runs, then a good ten kilometre. Schedule if possible. Tried to break my best time, not nearly so hot today but didn't succeed – 24:50.*

DECEMBER 2: *Ran a reverse July 27-route (7 km) in 25:40. New shoes are a little heavy.*

DECEMBER 3: *Terrible stomach bug. Could not run.*

What a way to celebrate a birthday.

DECEMBER 4: *Jogged, walked and sprinted ten kilometres. I am still weak from my stomach trouble, but things are looking up.*

DECEMBER 5: *No run. Still have stomach trouble.*

WEEKLY MILEAGE:

Approximately 25 kilometres.

> **DECEMBER 6:** *Ran a reverse July 27-route*
> *(7 km). I was nearly hit by a car. Apart from that*
> *incident, it was a good run, and I even enjoyed*
> *the climb up Bryanston Drive – 24:40.*

We runners must never forget to run defensively and be aware of traffic at all times. I always like to face oncoming traffic.

> **DECEMBER 7:** *Bad hay fever. Hay fever pills made*
> *my heart race but managed to run six kilometres.*

It can be a bad idea to run on medication.

> **DECEMBER 8:** *32:35 for my Brescia House route.*
> *Ideal running conditions, overcast and cool. Traffic a*
> *bit irritating. Four months later, almost to the day,*
> *I knocked 2 minutes, 50 seconds off my old time.*
>
> **DECEMBER 9:** *Time pressure. One*
> *quick four-kilometre run.*
>
> **DECEMBER 10:** *Ran the August 11-route*
> *(10 km) in 36:45. Over three minutes faster despite*
> *having to stop once to tie a loose shoelace.*

I still hadn't learnt to give my different runs names and route descriptions rather than refer clumsily to them by the date I first ran them. In later months, and once I had started to train with clubmates, runs would start to be named J.S.E., Parkview Golf Course, Sweat Shop, Wanderers, etc.

> **DECEMBER 11:** *Only had time for a short three-kilometre run. Quite stiff after the fast run yesterday.*

> **DECEMBER 12:** *Twenty-six kilometres with Roly in a little over one hour for ten kilometres. Sprinted the last kilometre to loosen my legs.*

My legs were not used to running for so long. As I became more experienced, I discovered that changing pace from time to time and running a couple of short sharp bursts can help to ease stiff legs.

WEEKLY MILEAGE:
Approximately 60 kilometres.

> **DECEMBER 13:** *Very easy three-kilometre run. Legs quite stiff after yesterday's run.*

> **DECEMBER 14:** *August 11-route again (10 km). Ideal, cool running conditions. Felt I was taking it easy but still beat my best time. Ran 36:30. Never really felt tired.*

DECEMBER 15: *Time problems again. Ran a fast five-kilometre. Quite tired afterwards.*

DECEMBER 16: *Brescia House run at 13:00 in hot, muggy weather. Cut it short by one kilometre (9 km). Battled up Bryanston Drive. Partying and lack of sleep last night didn't help.*

DECEMBER 17: *Brescia House run again. Hot late afternoon. Ran well but forgot to start my watch. I was pouring with sweat afterwards.*

DECEMBER 18: *Time problems. Only time for a fast three-kilometre run.*

DECEMBER 19: *July 27-route (7 km), met a Comrades runner on the road and enjoyed talking to him about the race. My right leg injury has been good for over a week now. Improved about a week ago and hasn't returned. Good, comfortable run.*

I wish I had recorded the name of the Comrades runner I chatted to. I would love to meet him again.

WEEKLY MILEAGE:
Approximately 50 kilometres.

DECEMBER 20: *Ran six kilometres on a new route.*

DECEMBER 21: *Played tennis all day. No time to run.*

DECEMBER 22: *Ran an eight-kilometre route to Brescia House. Quite strong, even enjoyed the long climb up Bryanston Drive. A little stiff after yesterday's tennis.*

A few years later I stopped playing any sport which could injure me or cause stiffness the next day.

DECEMBER 23: *Four-kilometre jog. Played tennis all day.*

I was still having fun playing tennis, and though running was important to me, it wasn't always the number one priority it would later become. A few years later, a Wimbledon champion would inspire and motivate me to win my first Comrades Marathon. In 1976, Swedish tennis player Björn Borg won the first of his five Wimbledon singles titles. The good-looking, long-haired Swede was a sensation; his popularity was similar to that of a pop star. I was a huge fan. I credit his 1980 epic victory over John McEnroe (considered by many to be the greatest Wimbledon final ever played) with inspiring me to win my first Comrades. Borg beautifully illustrated how deep you sometimes have to dig to achieve something momentous. That dark winter's evening in June I ran up Johannesburg's Oxford Road aware of the goosebumps on my arms and fantasising what it would take to win the Comrades Marathon. That run was the first step I took on my journey to the 1981 Comrades. Many years later I attended an exhibition tennis tournament at Sandton Square, where several former stars played for charity. Björn Borg was sitting a few seats in front of me, waiting for his turn to play. I wanted to thank him for inspiring me all those years ago, but he was surrounded by adoring fans, and I was too shy.

My tennis hero, Björn Borg, wins another Wimbledon title. (Getty Images)

DECEMBER 24: *Brescia House run. Used new running shorts, so light I had to check that they were still there! 33:16.*

Up until then, I had been running in black rugby shorts. Things were changing!

DECEMBER 25: *Family Christmas lunch. Too much eating and drinking. No run.*

DECEMBER 26: *July 27-route (7 km). Felt I was charging along. Equalled best time in 24:29.*

WEEKLY MILEAGE:

Approximately 35 kilometres.

DECEMBER 27: *Ran twenty-five kilometres with Roly. Very slowly, as usual. Never felt tired, but legs started to ache. Played tennis afterwards.*

DECEMBER 28: *Legs very stiff from yesterday's long run and tennis but ran three kilometres.*

DECEMBER 29: *Reverse July 27-route (7 km). Really enjoyed the run.*

DECEMBER 30: *No run.*
Holiday distractions.

DECEMBER 31: *Could only manage a three-kilometre run. New Year celebrations are leaning rather heavily on my running.*

I ran 206 kilometres in the seventh month of my training. With more free time over the holiday, I had unsurprisingly run my biggest monthly total since I started my Comrades journey earlier that year. The stage was perfectly set for an exciting 1977!

January 1977

JANUARY 1: *Ran a new route past Bryanston Post Office and back. Glorious running to greet the New Year. Coasted along and really enjoyed the run—about nine kilometres in 34:35.*

JANUARY 2: *Ran reverse July 27-route (7 km). Had a late night last night. Ran the route in 25:30.*

WEEKLY MILEAGE:

Approximately 55 kilometres.

JANUARY 3: *Post office run. New shoes and hot late afternoon – 33:45.*

JANUARY 4: *Post office run again. Felt almost perfect. Ran first half fast, then eased back – 33:00.*

JANUARY 5: *Reverse post office route. Slipped into a fast glide and ate up the miles. Finished in 33:25.*

JANUARY 6: *No Run.*

JANUARY 7: *Ran July 27-route (7 km). Unpleasant run. Felt jerky, uncoordinated and stiff. It was mind over matter and matter nearly won.*

JANUARY 8: *Reverse post office route again. Cool, stormy conditions. Headwind nearly brought me to a standstill. Ran a great time though – 32:50*

JANUARY 9: *Disastrous. Couldn't run. Put out of action by a bash and cut on my head. Running would have re-opened the cut.*

The evening before, I walked into a wall and cut my head badly. The wound did not require stitches, but the cut was painful and throbbing and was threatening to bleed again if I ran. Running injuries are not the only injuries that can interfere with our plans.

WEEKLY MILEAGE:
Approximately 40 kilometres.

JANUARY 10: *Head much better. Felt fine this morning and the weather was beautifully cool, so I decided to run. Ran the post office route with an extension past Sloane Centre. That made it ten kilometres, perhaps a little bit longer—about 41 minutes. Ran an extra three kilometres in the evening.*

JANUARY 11: *Ran seven kilometres.*

JANUARY 12: *Ran the reverse post office route (8.5 km) at midday but the conditions were perfect: Overcast and cool with a slight breeze. Time – 31:49. In race conditions, I am sure I could break 30 minutes.*

JANUARY 13: *I decided to run the 6.8 km-Bryanston Country Club route because of the danger of imminent rain and because I felt like a sprint and a crack at my personal best time of 23:20 on November 23 on this route. Cruised along and made that time look daft. The pace told as I climbed Bryanston Drive, but my early fast pace brought me a time of 21:10! I was fully extended, but in a race situation who knows?*

I had not yet heard of the term "p.b." which is so important to all runners, so I still spelt it out: personal best time. Interestingly, I understood that in a race situation, I could probably dig a little deeper.

JANUARY 14: *It's been a long time since I had such a ghastly run. Nothing was right. I think the past two days of fast running have drained me. I was tired very soon after starting, the miles got longer and longer, and the heat was incredible. 18:00 and it felt like the Sahara Desert. Also developed bad stomach cramps on the run. Post office run in 33:40 (8.5 km). I am pouring sweat.*

We all have "those" days. Not every run can be perfect.

JANUARY 15: *No run.*

JANUARY 16: *Post office run in 33:10 (8.5 km). Slight stomach problems.*

WEEKLY MILEAGE:

Approximately 50 kilometres.

JANUARY 17: *No run.*

JANUARY 18: *Ran the July 27-route (7 km). Pushed it most of the way. Enjoyed the run. Ran a little later in the afternoon. Not so hot – 24:30.*

JANUARY 19: *Post office run – 33:00 in ideal conditions (8.5 km).*

JANUARY 20: *Ran the reverse July 27-route (7 km). Last two kilometres in pouring rain. The rain was cooling but weighed my shoes down. Fastest time so far – 23:53.*

JANUARY 21: *Ran reverse post office route (8.5 km). Started slowly and enjoyed the run – 34:15.*

JANUARY 22: *Usual Saturday rush. Fast three-kilometre run.*

Social life interfering.

JANUARY 23: *No run.*

Social life definitely interfering again. Too much partying!

WEEKLY MILEAGE:
Approximately 30 kilometres.

JANUARY 24: *Longer run on a new route along Randburg main road to the bridge near Fourways and back home. Outward journey 25:00, back in 22:45. Twelve kilometres in 47:45.*

JANUARY 25: *Ran the July 27-route (7 km). Toiled along fighting the heat and terrible runner's guts – 25:57.*

JANUARY 26: *No run. Terrible stomach bug.*

JANUARY 27: *Ran January 24-route (Randburg to Fourways and back – 12 km) in 46:30. Cool day; overcast with a slight headwind on the return journey.*

JANUARY 28: *Ran reverse January 10-route (10 km). Jogged along happily in sunny but cool conditions. Never really felt I was running fast but pleased with ten kilometres in 38:00. Next month, the minimum distance of each run must be ten kilometres.*

I was starting to feel the pressure of a date with destiny in May of that year.

> **JANUARY 29**: *No run.*
>
> **JANUARY 30**: *Ran 20 kilometres with Roly. A chronic case of runner's guts after seven kilometres. Had to stop. Apart from this bush stop, it was a pleasant run in overcast conditions. Watched an official 32-kilometre race in progress while driving home. I must race soon!*

It happens to us all, and it would happen to me many times in the future. The pit stop/bush call of which I am most proud stopped me in full stride, but only briefly, while I was racing the 1980 Stellenbosch Marathon. I hid in a vineyard, lost a handful of seconds and still finished 3rd in 02:21:25.

I believe I witnessed the 1977 running of the Rand Athletic Club (R.A.C.) Tough One, which in those days was run in late January or early February. I still remember being awestruck by the sweating lead runners who were toiling up the long drag from Fourways to Randburg. A runner in a red and white hooped vest was leading. He was running powerfully. I had no idea I was watching Derek Preiss from Westville Athletic Club who had won the 1974 and 1975 Comrades Marathons. Interesting that I didn't enjoy being a spectator. "I must race soon". I wanted to be a participant. Years later, after leaving university, I would run for R.A.C. and win the Gunga Din Comrades team prize five times with my R.A.C. teammates. I would also run the Tough One fourteen times.

WEEKLY MILEAGE:

Approximately 60 kilometres.

> JANUARY 31: *Ran the July 27-route (7 km).*
> *Finished the month off with an enjoyable run.*
> *Held myself back in the beginning and then belted*
> *along in the last two kilometres or so – 25:05.*

During the eighth month, I ran 216 kilometres – another record month. I was delighted with my progress.

February 1977

FEBRUARY 1: *Beautiful run in the heat. Felt quite faint afterwards. January 24-route. Felt so good while running, turned in around 23:45. "Burned it" for the third quarter, then "vasbyted" the last quarter. (Interesting use of an Afrikaans expression for "endured" with an English ending!) Finished in 49 minutes or so for a hard, hilly 12 kilometres. Great start to the month.*

FEBRUARY 2: *January 10-route (10 km) in 38:05. Beautiful, still running conditions. Slightly stiff on the uphills.*

FEBRUARY 3: *Reverse January 10-route (10 km) in 39:05. The relatively long, fast runs over the last few days have taken their toll. I felt them as I ran along today. More beautiful running conditions – cool, still and overcast.*

FEBRUARY 4: *Tired and listless after a few hard days of running. Roly advised me to take a day off.*

It is important to listen to your body and to rest when you are unduly tired or stiff. It is also useful to listen to the advice of experienced runners. Roly was far more experienced than me and was almost like a coach. I valued his advice.

> **FEBRUARY 5**: *Reverse January 10-route (10 km). Not much fun – it was very hot and battled most of the way.*

Not every run is pleasant, and sometimes we have to grit our teeth and just get them done.

> **FEBRUARY 6**: *Ran 28 – 30 kilometres with Roly, at his pace. Fast last two kilometres. Legs stiff and feet sore towards the end.*

Many years later my mother told me that after my stepfather and I had shared several long training runs, Roly told her: "Bruce gets stronger the longer it gets. He could be a very good marathon runner".

WEEKLY MILEAGE:
Approximately 65 kilometres.

> **FEBRUARY 7**: *No run. Resting after longest run yet.*

> **FEBRUARY 8**: *University term commences. In the late afternoon, I ran for a second time with the Wits club members up Jan Smuts Avenue and*

> *around campus (4 km). Not as fast as I had feared.*
> *Comfortable breathing and running at talking pace.*

Even though I lived at home in Bryanston, my parents insisted that I should spend at least a year in a university residence so that I could lead a true university existence. They were right, and I truly value my years spent in residence.

At the commencement of the new term, I immediately joined the Wits University Marathon Club, one of the most important steps I could take, second only in importance to the first running steps I took in June the year before. In South Africa, we are obliged to belong to a running club in order to participate in races and to obtain a licence number. A typical distance race will have runners participating from many different clubs, all sporting their club colours. I proudly wore the blue and gold colours of my university for several years. Most importantly, new club members are advised and "coached" by the experienced runners. I was to learn so much from my fellow Wits runners in the next few weeks. There were very few athletics coaches in those days, and no Comrades Marathon coaches at all, so my experienced club mates became my coaches. I absorbed all the knowledge and experience I could from them. The Wits Marathon Club had a respected running tradition, and when I joined the club, names like Levick, Parry, Gardener, and Chamberlain were spoken of almost in hushed tones.

I ran four kilometres with the residence's freshmen around campus at a fast pace.

I was a senior student resident in College House Men's Residence. For a week or so, the first-year students (freshmen) in residence were advised to experience an orientation programme so that they could learn the ropes and understand the traditions of the residence. Nothing was compulsory, but those who wished to could run every day. We seniors took turns to lead the runs.

One evening during orientation week, a very solemn ceremony took place in the residence quadrangle. We residents had to strip off and don our academic gowns and nothing else. While we stood in semi-naked silence in the quadrangle, one brave soul volunteered or was chosen to become a member of "The Dance Club", an exclusive club of reckless residents who had managed to down a bottle of port in 25 seconds and were able to hold the contents down for ten minutes. For most challengers, this was an impossible task, but in the 1977 orientation year, we had a new hero and member of The Dance Club. His name is known to me, but he shall remain anonymous as he is now a practising dentist in Sandton somewhere and is a pillar of society. I have no idea why the ceremony was called "The Dance Club" as there was no dancing whatsoever, but in celebration of a new member of the club we had to run around the outer circumference of Wits campus, once again clad only in our academic gowns. It's an interesting fact that while running at full speed, an academic gown offers no modesty protection at all. It flies out behind the runner like a Batman or Superman cape. The route we had to run was past the Sunnyside Women's Residence, out onto Jan Smuts Avenue, along Empire Road and then up Yale Road back to the residence via the planetarium. If we were able to complete this run, we were entitled to become members of another exclusive club called "The Bare-Bottomed Harriers". Predictably someone had tipped off the ladies in Sunnyside Residence, and they were standing in the street outside their residence to cheer us on, but sadly someone had also tipped off the police, and they were waiting for us as we spilled out onto Jan Smuts Avenue. Witsies were always a favourite target of the police, and these policemen had arrived with the full arsenal of weaponry. They were laden with handcuffs and riot sticks and were supported by police trucks and snarling dogs. We fled across the campus, academic gowns streaming out behind us, with the police in hot pursuit. I doubt that I have ever run so fast. I eventually took cover behind a large pot plant outside the science laboratory. Under cover of darkness, I sneaked back to the residence with a few mates while police torches probed behind every corner.

The next day the Dean of Residence was not amused that he had to go to the Hillbrow Police Station to post bail for several cold and scantily clad students who had been caught and arrested. I don't recall there being another Dance Night-ceremony in my time at university.

> **FEBRUARY 9**: *Ran four kilometres with freshmen again. The University's orientation programme interfered with the Wits club run.*

To attract members to the marathon club during orientation week, the senior club members organised a relay race around the university's central campus. Each runner had to down a glass of beer, then run a fast two-kilometre lap before handing on to the next runner. This was repeated several times. Needless to say, the athletics club attracted quite a few new runners, and towards the end, the event became a little chaotic.

> **FEBRUARY 10:** *Ran 9.5 miles (15 km) with Wits club. Met Jax Snyman and John "Squirrel" Bush.*

This run served as my introduction to the club. It turned out to be a baptism of fire, but I conducted myself well. It was a legendary run that Jax still talks about. Wits runners met every afternoon at the squash courts at the Empire Road end of the university campus. The senior Witsies had planned a fast-paced training run, and then I spoiled the party by arriving to run with them. They were concerned they were going to have to nurse the new guy (me) around the route. But they soon realised I could look after myself quite adequately. To this day Jax still says he found himself hanging on to the fast pace and as the kilometres clicked by, he became more concerned about himself than about the "new guy". Jacobus Christoffel Snyman (Jax) and John Bush were to become great friends and wonderful sources of advice and encouragement.

> **FEBRUARY 11:** *Sore throat, so no run.*

I suspect I had a sore throat from partying until late the night before with the College House freshmen in a very smoky Devonshire Hotel's pub. The Devonshire Pub, known affectionately as "The Dev" was a popular watering hole with students in those days.

In my first year in residence, I earned enormous status with my fellow residents because I was able to become one of the few male students to have a bath in the

Sunnyside Women's Residence. Now men were allowed into Sunnyside but only as far as the reception room at the entrance. Here they could wait for their date for the evening, but always under the eagle-eyes of the extremely ferocious "Machine Gun Maggie". I am sorry to admit that after all these years I cannot remember "Machine Gun Maggie's" real name, but I haven't forgotten that she was a formidable gatekeeper and no one could sneak past her.

However, one evening I dressed up in a dress and heels, smeared on some make-up and left my long hair hanging loose. With the help of some compliant lady residents, I cowered in the middle of their group of chatting and laughing ladies. They caused a distraction with their noise, and I was able to deftly ease past Maggie at the entrance of Sunnyside and then shoot into the bathroom, run a very shallow bath, splash some water over myself and steal the bath caddy. (We had to produce proof that we had had that bath.) Escaping from Sunnyside Residence was more terrifying than entering, but I simply bolted out of the door and fled into the night. I was a hero in College House Residence for several weeks afterwards. The bath caddy was placed alongside various trophies in the residence's trophy cabinet. A few months later, a group of us kidnapped the pet duck from Sunnyside's lily pond. But that is another story ...

> **FEBRUARY 12**: *Even with a bad cold, I decided to run. Ran six to seven kilometres on my own. I really felt it, especially when I tried to turn on the pace. Hoping to be better soon.*

> FEBRUARY 13: *Ran 21 miles with Guy Nottingham*
> *from Wits to the Syringa Spa Resort (now the*
> *Avianto Estate) for Wits Residence function*
> *in 02:40. Felt I could have gone faster.*

Guy Nottingham is still running and has run several Comrades Marathons, has completed an Iron Man or two and has run the Washie 100-miler in recent years.

WEEKLY MILEAGE:

Approximately 50 kilometres.

> FEBRUARY 14: *Eight-mile run with the club. I had*
> *slight stomach pains and could feel yesterday's*
> *long run. My debilitating emotional problems*
> *with Elaine are also showing themselves.*

Ironically, it was Valentine's Day. This was an awful time in my life as the first truly serious relationship I had ever had, began to unravel rapidly. I found it hard to run with a dull ache in my heart, and running anywhere near Northcliff, where I had run so often in happier times, was hideous. At night, the light winking on top of the Northcliff water tower used to haunt me. A few days earlier I had bought an album by Hatfield and the North, *The Rotters' Club,* and to this day I cannot listen to any song from that album, but particularly the song "Didn't Matter Anyway" without sad memories. The Yes song, "And You and I" from the album *Close To The Edge* also remind me of sad days. But, running also saved me. It was my rock and my best friend, and it did so much for my otherwise battered self-esteem. It is important to realise that running, racing and training do not happen in isolation and that the stresses and strains of life itself can take their toll.

Elaine Proctor

FEBRUARY 15: *Twelve kilometres with Wits club. I could feel the last three hard runs. Legs stiff and left ankle was particularly sore—very heavy heart.*

FEBRUARY 16: *Much better today. Met some more Wits club members. Ran the Parkview Golf Course route (10 km). Beginning to ease off for my first race, the Springs Striders 32 kilometre, on Sunday.*

Worth noting that in those days the golf course was open for runners and walkers. It was not fenced in, and there was no security. It was a lovely soft, green grass journey out, but quite tough coming back. The Springs Striders 32-kilometre (20 miles) was one of the major races and stepping stones on the journey to the Comrades, and it was an essential part of the build-up. It was to be my first formal race and was to teach me no end of a lesson about pacing.

> FEBRUARY 17: *Ten kilometres on the golf course route with the club. That is enough for me. Could feel the efforts of the last few days and poor sleep from emotional problems.*

Sleep does not come easily when you have a broken heart.

I am taking two days rest before the race. A sensible decision. I always like to rest for a couple of days before a major race.

> FEBRUARY 18: *No run. Resting for Striders.*
>
> FEBRUARY 19: *No run. Resting for Striders. Eating carbohydrates.*

A few weeks later, I was to use the Saltin diet, a more rigorous form of carbohydrate loading for my first Comrades. (Note: More on the diet below – see May 24.)

FEBRUARY 20: *Striders! First 20-mile/32-kilometre race. Incredible test. Incredible race. 1 300 runners. I remember being impressed by the runners whose tracksuit tops were covered in race badges.*

Every race awarded badges in those days. Before the start of the race, we left our bags under a tree near the start, and when we returned, our bags were still there. Inside the bags were our tracksuits, beers, wallets, and car keys. No one had stolen them! That certainly would not happen today!

*I ran through halfway (10 miles/16 km) in 59:50. After a terrible battle up the hills in the last quarter of the race, I finished 103*rd *out of 1 300 runners with a time of 02:05:40.*

I learnt so many lessons in this first race and probably the single most important lesson of all, the one that would determine my racing strategy for the next 20 years. Clearly, I started too fast, and my first 16 kilometres were too fast. I lost almost six minutes in the second half, and it was a long, bitter struggle. I set off with my clubmates and training partners – runners like Jax Snyman and Dave Johnson – but I overestimated my ability. I was, after all, a raw novice. I thought that because I had stayed with my friends in training, I could easily match them in races. I was mistaken. After a few kilometres, I realised I was hanging on, and then I was on my own. I was proud of the fact that I had not walked, and that I had fought hard. I remember two kind Springs Striders runners came past me and encouraged me: "Come on, Witsie, you can do this." Jax Snyman and several other Witsies soundly beat me, but my teammates were all delighted with my run. The following week my performance was mentioned in the *Wits Student* newspaper: "New runner, Bruce Fordyce, had a memorable run finishing in ..."

> **WEEKLY MILEAGE:**
> **Approximately 75 kilometres.**

FEBRUARY 21: *Missed. Very stiff after yesterday's race.*

Not surprising after the effort I had put in the morning before.

FEBRUARY 22: *Ten kilometres with the club along the extended golf course route. Right leg giving me trouble. Might have to take a day off again. Very stiff and sore, but my stamina is improving.*

FEBRUARY 23: *Decided to skip my run again. I still haven't fully recovered from Sunday.*

FEBRUARY 24: *This is ridiculous. My right calf is still giving me trouble. I ran eight miles with the club today, and after three miles it started playing up. Towards the end of the training run, every pace I took was agony. I think I will have to skip tomorrow's run then run five kilometres on Saturday, six kilometres on Sunday, etc. This is bad for my Comrades schedule!*

Even today, I can still remember the frustration of that injury. There I was, trying to train for my first Comrades and I was injured, and it was late February already! In later years I would understand that an injury in February is of no consequence. In fact, it's probably a blessing in disguise. But in February 1977 it was a disaster. However, any injury that gets more painful as the run progresses is certainly one that needs attention.

> FEBRUARY 25: *Resting due to injury.*

> FEBRUARY 26: *Still resting due to injury.*

> FEBRUARY 27: *Ran a slow eight-kilometre with the club which included the steep Jan Smuts Avenue climb. I could feel my calf muscle as I ran, but it wasn't nearly as bad as the last run. It has improved.*

Rather like a bruise, this post-race injury just needed time to fade away. If I was given ten rand for every occasion I have toiled up the steep Jan Smuts Avenue hill, I would be a millionaire now.

WEEKLY MILEAGE:
Approximately 30 kilometres.

> FEBRUARY 28: *Ran eight miles with the club. I could still feel my calf twinging. It's there, loitering with intent and waiting to give me more trouble, but I favoured it all the way, and it was much better than on February 24.*

In the ninth month since my training started, I ran 250 kilometres. I had now run my first race and had struggled with my first serious injury. Despite February being a short month, I had run my furthest monthly total in training mileage. Most importantly, I had joined the Wits University Running Club and was now training with other club members and was receiving good, wise advice.

March 1977

> MARCH 1: *Ran eight miles with the club across the golf course. Did some fartlek with Jax and Dave Johnson but then eased off because I could still feel that my right calf was not happy. I could feel the odd twinge.*

"Fartlek" is the Swedish word for "speed play". It is an informal and fun way to get some faster running done while avoiding the rigorous discipline of track sessions and accurately timed sprint repetitions. It is particularly suited to golf courses. After a reasonable warm-up, runners run fast surges for as long as they like and as far as they like. In between each surge, they jog while recovering. This they repeat several times, once again as many times as they like.

"Ok team, let's sprint to that tree," or "Ready everyone? Let's surge for five lampposts." That's fartlek for you.

> MARCH 2: *Now I am really into it! Woke up early to run five kilometres. Felt terrific after the run and a shower. In the afternoon, ran ten kilometres with the club.*

For the first time, apart from some light-hearted running during the playful first few days of the university term,

I ran twice in one day. In later years, two sessions a day
would become essential in order to run a 200-kilometre
week and to develop the fitness to break five and a half
hours in the Comrades Marathon.

I have always believed the correct training build-up
to Comrades starts at the end of February/beginning of
March. This is the time to get serious and to increase
training mileage. April is the most important Comrades
training month. In later years, many top coaches would
agree with me, including the very influential sports scientist, Tim Noakes. We can only sustain eight to ten weeks
of intense training and, allowing for a two-week training
taper to race day, this makes the beginning of March
(autumn in South Africa) the time to work hard. What has
happened before, in January and February, is not critical. Of
course, back in 1977, I was simply following my gut instinct
and the advice of some of my fellow student runners.

MARCH 3: *Surprisingly, woke up feeling stiff, so
skipped the morning run. Evening run with the
club – eight miles with some hard sprinting at the end.*

MARCH 4: *Morning run of five kilometres.
Cool, beautiful morning – kept up a brisk
pace. Six miles in the evening.*

MARCH 5: *No run.*

MARCH 6: *Overslept. Only time for a five-mile jog.*

WEEKLY MILEAGE:
Approximately 80 – 90 kilometres.

"Weekly mileage approximately 80 – 90 kilometres." Perhaps one of the questions I am asked most frequently is: "What is the least amount of training I can do to complete the Comrades Marathon?" This is a very open-ended question because it depends on the aim of the runner. Is he or she aiming for a gold medal, or a last-minute finish before the final cut-off gun? Is he or she a genetically gifted runner? The answers to those varied goals are completely different. However, when pushed I like to advise that every runner should try to cover the Comrades distance of 90 kilometres in the course of a training week, at least a few times before race day.

> MARCH 7: *Twelve-kilometre run with the club.*
> *Went over J.M.T. course. Racing it on Thursday.*
> *It is going to be a tough race. I turned up the*
> *pace at the end to pull clear of our group.*

The John Morris Trophy (J.M.T.) was a cup awarded to the best Witsie at this monthly cross-country/road 12-kilometre run. It was run on an extremely tough course, which included running up the steep roads behind Melville Koppies and then plunging down the stony Melville Koppies paths. It finished up Empire Road and back onto the Wits cricket field at the Bozzoli Stadium. John Morris was a former chairman of the athletics club, and the trophy was meant to help us get fit for the coming Transvaal cross-country season. I was never awarded the trophy!

> MARCH 8: *Five kilometres in the morning, quite fast. In the evening, ran the sixteen-kilometre February 10-route. Fast pace. Slower runners chose a different route. Finished first home with Jax Snyman and Dave Johnson. Lower right Achilles tendon gave me trouble. Again, feeling quite drained from emotional problems.*

Sadly, the pain of a relationship coming to an end was still taking its toll. But I was determined to let running help to restore some dignity and sense of control in my life. In many ways running was one of my best coping mechanisms at that sad time.

> MARCH 9: *Skipped morning run. Wary of my tendon. Eight miles with Jax at a fast pace in the evening.*

> MARCH 10: *Seven miles with the club on a dark and wet evening. Good run. Could feel twinges in both Achilles's tendons but not serious.*

> MARCH 11: *Six comfortable miles on my own. Only pushed the last mile. Slight headwind but cool, overcast weather.*

> MARCH 12: *No run.*

> MARCH 13: *Ran 32 kilometres in cool, misty, early morning conditions. Legs became quite stiff as the run*

wore on but felt good. Ran 02:25 for 32 kilometres.
Could easily have pushed on for the full marathon.

The Wits Marathon Club was going to race the Vaal Marathon a week later, so I was probably trying to psych myself up for the challenge of my first 42 kilometres standard marathon. I intended the Vaal Marathon to be my qualifying marathon for the Comrades. In those days runners had to break four and a half hours for a standard marathon in order to qualify for the Comrades.

WEEKLY MILEAGE:

Approximately 85 kilometres.

MARCH 14: *Rest day after a long 32-kilometre run.*

MARCH 15: *J.M.T. tough seven and a half-mile race.*
Ran too cautiously. Ran with George Mende (02:01 at
Striders), then he dropped back. I was very fresh at
the end. Should have run with Jax who was finishing
with the leaders when I ran onto the Wits cricket field.
Finished fourth in 41:50, fifty metres behind Jax.

MARCH 16: *Thirteen kilometres around Brixton*
with the club in cold conditions. We pushed the last
two miles home. Really hurtled along. That must
be the last hard run before the Vaal Marathon.

I was beginning to understand the concept of tapering and resting before a major marathon effort. With two or three days to go before a major marathon, there is nothing any runner can do to get stronger and fitter, but there is plenty that same runner can do to get to the starting line tired, stiff and over-trained.

> MARCH 17: *Boozy lunch with fellow students in The Dev. Twelve kilometres with the club with four beers in my stomach. Wasn't good for me, especially the last hectic three kilometres. Burped and belched my way along.*

Not a good idea. Alcohol and running do not mix. Well, they can do ... if you get the order correct. Running comes first!

> MARCH 18 AND 19: *Rest days for the marathon.*

I have always preferred a couple of days of complete rest before a major effort—three days for an ultra.

> MARCH 20: *My first marathon: the Vaal Marathon in Vereeniging.*

This race was and still is run on a very flat course past vast mealie (maize) fields. It is usually hot and dry.

I paced myself far better than at Striders. Drank Game (a sports drink) and water. Tore through the field in the second half. Far faster second half. Passed through eight kilometres in 00:33. Ten miles (16 km) in 01:06 and twenty miles in 02:07. Finished 24th in 02:44. Sore legs, and stomach problems after-

wards. Bronze medal, badge and I qualified for the South African Marathon Championships. Great run. Great fun.

Afterwards, I called it "a day of triumph". I treasured that bronze medal, and I still have it. For days afterwards I left my medal lying conspicuously on my mantlepiece where I hoped as many people as possible would see it.

1977 Vaal Marathon badge and medal.

Having learnt my lesson at Springs Striders, I now accepted and understood which tactics would work best for me when racing major marathons in the future. I learnt to "start like a coward and finish like a hero". This tactic would be even more successful in ultramarathons. Importantly, on an out-and-back section of that Vaal Marathon course, I was given a good look at the leading runners. Two things surprised me. One was that the leaders were not light years ahead of me. The other was that they were tired and struggling. They too were human! Two years later, I won the Vaal Marathon in 02:28:13.

The last 100 metres of my first marathon,
the 1977 Vaal Marathon.

I cannot recommend this cautious approach to racing more. It works particularly well for novices setting off into the unknown. Starting cautiously ensures a strong finish, and there is nothing more motivating for runners than to be running the last kilometres strongly and to be passing other runners at the end of the race. To ensure a cautious start, running should feel comfortable and easy in the early kilometres. Conversation should come easily, and the kilometres should click past steadily. The overwhelming sensation should be of pent-up energy that is waiting to explode but is released instead like slow steam from a kettle. It is a hard skill to learn or teach, but the dominant emotion on the start line should one of fear. Remember, the meek shall inherit the Earth.

> **WEEKLY MILEAGE:**
>
> **Approximately 80 kilometres.**

> **MARCH 21**: *Rest day. Stiff and I have a few blisters. As from tomorrow, I must start running again. Major build-up for the next important race.*

The Korkie 56-kilometre was a month away. Following my success at the Vaal Marathon, I was impatient to pin on some racing numbers again.

> **MARCH 22**: *An easy 12 kilometres with the club. Could feel Sunday's marathon, so it was a good thing the pace was slow. Blisters on my toes are giving me a little trouble.*

Blisters on my toes and painful black toenails were problems I was to encounter in many marathons in the future. I think I recall losing eight toenails in the 1977 Comrades. In later years I learnt to cut open the toe-box of my running shoes so that my toes were free of any pressure. This was a trick I learnt from the old-timers. I noticed many photographs of runners with early model running shoes with their toes poking out of holes cut in the front of their shoes. It didn't look good cosmetically, and my running shoes always looked like a butcher had been at work on them, but the surgery worked, and in future years it saved many toenails.

> MARCH 23: *A hard ten-miler in sixty-three minutes with Jax, Dale and Hamish. Legs still stiff.*

Dale Rogers and Hamish Gilfillan were both studying law at Wits University. Both were to become good running and university friends. In fact, Hamish was both a friend and a running rival during that first year. He had finished one position and a few seconds ahead of me at the Vaal Marathon.

> MARCH 24: *Five kilometres in the morning. A fast, tough run. I can still feel the marathon. Legs quite sore and back of knees tight. Decided to skip the evening run.*

I hadn't yet learnt that a hard marathon requires an equally dedicated recovery phase.

> MARCH 25: *Five kilometres in the morning. Sore legs – very tight and had to battle. Struggled this evening as well. Ran the February 10-route (16 km) with Jax, Dale and Hamish. I was fighting after two miles, and my legs are too sore. I think I must rest again.*

> MARCH 26: *Rest day.*

> MARCH 27: *Twenty-five mile run with the club.*
> *Incredibly hilly route. I wasn't ever very tired,*
> *but my legs were quite sore, particularly my left*
> *hip. I was feeling good at the finish, though. We*
> *took about four hours to run the forty kilometres*
> *with frequent stops for the slower guys.*

WEEKLY MILEAGE:

Approximately 95 kilometres.

> MARCH 28: *Rest day.*
>
> MARCH 29: *J.M.T. race from Wits. Started*
> *too quickly and battled in the second half.*
> *Didn't ever feel good. Passed by George (42:25)*
> *and Dave Scott. Finished 6th in 42:55.*
>
> MARCH 30: *Twelve kilometres around*
> *Johannesburg Wilds with the club.*

The Wilds is a rocky, hilly park and has some rigorous climbs, and we ran fast.

> *Twinges from my right calf, but nothing serious since I*
> *will be resting for Sunday's race from tomorrow. After*
> *that, I will concentrate on the Korkie and the Comrades.*

> MARCH 31: *Last five kilometres morning run before Sunday's race. Tried to run fast but felt stale and over-trained. Two day's rest should see me right.*

During the tenth month since I started my training, I ran 359 kilometres. In keeping with my conviction that specific Comrades training should start at the beginning of March, I had substantially increased the quality of my training. I had also run my first marathon!

April 1977

APRIL 1: *Rest day.*

As an English major at university, the poetry of the great T.S. Eliot was part of my syllabus. At the time, we English students were studying one of the most important poems of the 20th century, Eliot's masterpiece "The Waste Land", and I remember thinking that the famous opening words of the poem were so appropriate for all Comrades runners: "April is the cruellest month ..."

The poem often has references to the quest for the Holy Grail, and for runners, the Comrades finisher's medal is the ultimate holy grail. April is indeed the cruellest month for Comrades runners, and in order to earn that coveted medal, runners must endure a very tough month of training in April.

APRIL 2: *Rest day.*

APRIL 3: *Twenty-kilometre Winners II Road Run. Paced the race well except for the finish in town. I thought there was over a kilometre to run when in fact there were only two city blocks. Finished far too*

> *fresh. Two major climbs up Jan Smuts Avenue and*
> *Houghton Drive, but I was strong on the hills.*

Houghton Drive and Jan Smuts Avenue are two of the major hills in hilly Johannesburg.

I had sore shins on some of the climbs. 39th in 67:30. Wits University won the second-team prize of R150. Teams of ten runners, so we young students each received R15. I was the eighth home for Wits.

This was the first prize money I ever received. This race was used to promote a film called Winners II (My Way II), starring the late Joe Stewardson and various South African actors. It was organised by the late Ivor Lazerson who was one of the great characters of South African road running and became chairman of the South African Road Running Association. My stepfather, Roly, also ran and finished.

> **WEEKLY MILEAGE:**
> **Approximately 50 kilometres.**

> **APRIL 4:** *Twelve kilometres golf course*
> *run with club. Wanted to run further but*
> *would have missed Residence supper!*

> **APRIL 5:** *Thirteen-kilometre run with the club*
> *around the Brixton Tower. Slow at first but*
> *quick run home. Tomorrow I start morning*
> *runs again. I am feeling loose and fit now.*

> APRIL 6: *Morning five kilometres at a brisk pace.*
> *Raced the morning traffic up Empire Road.*

I loved showing off in front of traffic by running as fast as I could.

Evening nine and a half-miler with the club. Bompas Road and back with a stiff climb up Big Jan Smuts Avenue. We finished in just over an hour, so we weren't messing around.

All club runs started and finished at the old university squash courts on Empire Road.

> APRIL 7: *Missed the run. Social life interfered.*

Following my traumatic break-up, I was trying to get out as much as possible, and my friends were dragging me to parties in the hope I would meet someone else. My mate David jokingly called it "shopping around for a replacement"!

> APRIL 8: *A ten-mile run on my own, but a fierce*
> *storm brewed up, and I had to cut my run short.*

About eight miles in driving rain, I've always found that starting in pouring rain is awful, but if it starts raining when you're already out on your run, it isn't so bad. I am, however, always concerned about lightning, particularly Johannesburg's ferocious and dangerous Highveld lightning, and then I seek shelter immediately.

APRIL 9: *At home again in Bryanston. Ran the January 24-route (12 km) on my own. Had to battle against sore shins in my right leg. I was really carrying that leg. Still beat my best time by 20 seconds – 45:30.*

APRIL 10: *Thirteen-kilometre run out towards Randburg. Leg a pain, but it got better as I ran. Mum picked me up afterwards.*

I can never adequately express my gratitude for the support I received from my family. My mother, in particular, believed in me from the earliest days and offered me so much encouragement and support. She has said she is very proud of my achievements as a runner but has never quite forgiven me for not winning ten Comrades Marathons.

WEEKLY MILEAGE:
Approximately 80 kilometres.

APRIL 11: *Ran 18 kilometres past Riversands Farm seconded by Mum. Some excellent hill climbing. My legs were stiff in the beginning, but they improved nicely as the run progressed, and I was feeling strong when I had to stop. My Comrades numbers have arrived in the post. I am Comrades number 2403. The big day is a month and a half away.*

I had no idea how significant the random number 2403 would become in my life. It has become my magic number, my lucky charm, and a number of which I am immensely proud. I would kill if I saw anyone else wearing it at Comrades.

> **APRIL 12**: *Ten-mile run with the club. Stamina was great, but my legs were terrible. Every possible sinew, tendon and muscle that could ache below my knee ached. Quite painful at the end.*

At times we all experience horrible runs. This was one of those runs that are best forgotten.

> **APRIL 13**: *Easy six or seven miles with Rob Bray (reading Architecture at Wits University). Took it easy all the way. My legs were giving me trouble. We chatted the whole way. At the moment, it's my Achilles tendon that is the biggest problem.*

Everyone gets niggles and slight problems in the build-up to Comrades. These need to be carefully monitored.

> **APRIL 14**: *Emmarentia ten-miler with the club. Slow, easy start – fast finish. Felt great the whole way. Not a hint of trouble from my legs. Was moving very easily at the end.*
>
> **APRIL 15**: *Fourteen kilometres or so on my own. Ran very strongly up the hills and then glided down the back of them. On the straights, I sprinted some sections and then eased back. Could feel yesterday's run.*

That morning, word filtered through the residence's corridors in hushed, secretive whispers that there was going to be a "special" movie showing for members of the residence. We were told to bring 50 cents and meet quietly in the common room. We were also warned not to tell a soul. Now South Africa was a very conservative Calvinistic country in those days, and many artistic activities and intellectual pursuits were forbidden by law. Consider that the great Sixto "Sugarman" Rodriguez's album, *Cold Fact*, was banned, as was the song "American Pie" by Don MacLean. It was banned because of the lines: *"And the three men I admire most, The Father, Son and the Holy Ghost, they caught the last train to the coast, the day the music died ..."* Obviously all forms of pornography were banned. The closest glimpse we might have of nudity would be *Scope* magazine's monthly photograph of a topless Miss Scottburgh wearing two strategically positioned stars. Macabrely, these bikini photos would usually be printed opposite a photo of a flame-throwing crisped "SWAPO terrorist", dangling lifeless and smoking from the cockpit of his smashed Soviet tank.

"Miss Scottburgh sends her love to all our boys on the border, who are clearly teaching the enemy no end of a lesson", the caption would read.

Even the devoutly Christian residents were gathered outside the common room that night, joining the rest of us speaking in muffled tones, clutching our money and trembling with excitement at the thought of our first blue movie. Imagine the collective horror and disappointment when the film began, and this text swept diagonally across the screen, seemingly drifting into infinity: "A long time ago, in a galaxy far, far away ..." What sort of film was this?

we pondered. Harrison Ford sounded like a slightly risqué screen name, but Carrie Fisher? That was a rubbish name for a blue movie star. Also, none of us were really keen to gaze at a scantily clad Alec Guinness. Slowly it dawned on us that we weren't going to see even a few seconds of smut, but we were going to be treated to one of the most astonishing visual treats of our young lives. It is difficult now to describe the impact the first *Star Wars* movie had on cinema back in 1977. It was quite simply astonishing! We are all sightly jaded now by the stream of *Star Wars* movies that have been released since 1977, but that evening, we watched a bootleg copy of one of the most extraordinary films ever made. For us young students, Han Solo (Harrison Ford) was the coolest hero we could imagine. (Raffish, cheeky and arrogantly confident, Solo was our favourite character.) Luke Skywalker's attack against the Death Star in his X-Wing fighter drew gasps and cheers and the bar scene in a Mos Eisley cantina filled with aliens described as "a wretched hive of scum and villainy" was unforgettable.

APRIL 16: *Just one five-kilometre loosening-up run.*

Late to bed the night before.

APRIL 17: *Ran home from the university. Comfortable run, which I really enjoyed. Cruised up the hills and even the steep Peter Place road wasn't unbearable. I am not doing enough mileage, though.*

Like all novice runners, you always think you should be training harder and the closer race day gets, the more worried you become!

> **WEEKLY MILEAGE:**
> **Approximately 90 kilometres.**

> APRIL 18: *Ran a steady nine miles with the club.*
> *Most of them turned back. (They ran the Bergville*
> *Marathon yesterday.) Dale, Jax, Jean and I carried on.*

Jean Leger is the fellow university resident who first
inspired me to run the Comrades many months earlier.
The Bergville/Arthur Creswell Memorial Race is a
52 – 54-kilometre ultramarathon, run from Bergville
to Ladysmith in KwaZulu-Natal in the foothills of the
beautiful Drakensberg Mountains. I would go on to run
seven Bergville races in later years.

> APRIL 19: *J.M.T. Club race. Despite a small field, I*
> *ran my best time of 41:04 (12 km). The pace at the*
> *start was a little slower, and this seems to be the*
> *answer. Hamish beat Jax by a few seconds, but I*
> *stayed in contact with them. We three left the others*
> *far behind. I am feeling a bit drained, so I am going*
> *to take it easy until Sunday's Korkie Marathon.*

> APRIL 20: *A light eight-kilometre run. Waiting for*
> *Sunday's race. I could feel the J.M.T. run in my legs.*

> APRIL 21: *A nine-kilometre run in intense*
> *heat. I haven't sweated like this for ages despite*
> *taking it very easy. Tomorrow similar.*

APRIL 22: *A eight-kilometres light jog. Took it very easy.*

APRIL 23: *Resting, so no run.*

As with the Striders 32-kilometre and the Vaal Marathon, I favoured a good training taper for every hard race. This would be especially true of the Comrades Marathon.

APRIL 24: *Pieter Korkie 53.5 km Marathon. Started easily again. Field of just below 1 000. Ran second half faster than the first half. 32 kilometres in 02:14 and 42 kilometres in 02:55. Legs very sore towards the end but ran along with Louis van Huysteen from the Police Athletic Club and Caspar Greeff from R.A.C. I passed some notable runners like John Bush, Geoff Deeny, (winner of the 1977 Vaal Marathon), Dennis Morrison (five-time winner of the Korkie) and Tommy Malone (1966 Comrades winner). Finished in 03:38. Brilliantly seconded by Mum and David. Won a beautiful Korkie silver medal for breaking four hours, a Korkie cloth badge and a Korkie beer mug.*

My 1977 Peter Korkie Marathon silver medal and badge.

The Pieter Korkie Marathon was a 33 – 35-mile race that was South Africa's second oldest ultramarathon and probably South Africa's second most important ultra after the Comrades. Pieter Korkie was an outstanding distance runner who was killed by a car while out training. At the time there were other 50 – 56-kilometre races in South Africa such as the Bergville in KZN and the Jock-of-the Bushveld in Mpumalanga. There was also a relatively new and interesting race in Cape Town which was becoming more prominent called the Two Oceans. However, aside from the Comrades, at the time, the Korkie was easily the most prestigious ultra. It was also a logical stepping-stone en route to the Comrades. The men's and women's lists of Korkie champions reads like the who's who of distance running in South Africa. I am delighted that eight years after running this first Korkie, I added my name to that list of winners. In addition to being ideally positioned on the racing calendar so that it served its purpose as a stepping-stone to Comrades, it was also the perfect dress rehearsal run. Though the Korkie had several different starting and finishing venues over the years (that 1977 Korkie started at Fountains Valley in Pretoria and ended on the sports fields at Jeppe Quondam Club in Bedfordview), it was essentially a run from Pretoria to Germiston. The race was affectionately known as the "slow poison race" because most of the route was run on a slight uphill or flat pull to Germiston. The race had little charisma, offered, plain and boring scenery (apart from beautiful stands of colourful cosmos flowers) and few spectators. Yet it was considered an essential part of any Comrades build-up. Old-timers expounded the wisdom that "if you have a good Korkie, your Comrades will also be successful". There was a formula, which I have forgotten, where you could ex-trapolate your Comrades time from your Korkie time and be accurate to within ten minutes. The fact that this myth-ical formula existed indicated the high regard in which the Korkie was held. Following my first run in 1977, I was to run it a further 14 times. Sadly, the race no longer exists, having succumbed to a combination of ever-increasing traffic volumes on the route and the competition of other more exciting events.

I was now completely hooked on running, and I remember being delighted with my Korkie silver medal. In many ways, those old amateur days had their own magic. Louis van Huysteen from the Police Athletic Club towed me through the last 12 kilometres, "Come on you long-haired Wits University communist; you can do this," he cajoled me, and he continued to urge me not to walk. We crossed the finish line together in joint 30th position. That year, the Korkie awarded special beer mugs to the top 30 finishers. Louis took the last top-30 beer mug and handed it to me, "This was your first ultra, Witsie. You deserve this."

> **WEEKLY MILEAGE:**
> **Approximately 105 kilometres.**

My first 100-kilometre week of training and racing. In later years I would sometimes run more than double this distance in training, but it was a significant milestone at the time.

> APRIL 25: *Legs sore and stiff. No run.*
>
> APRIL 26: *Ran an easy seven kilometres. Joints sore and stiff, but I was strong on all the hills. Still ran 18:55 on the January 20-route in 23:53. My time on July 27 for the same route was 26:20.*

I was clearly a much fitter and stronger runner. One of the magical benefits of the old Korkie race was that despite its distance, recovery was always fairly rapid after the race. Perhaps it was because the Korkie's course was slightly uphill or flat for most of its 50 plus kilometres that ensured that our legs didn't quite take the pounding they had to endure in so many other distance races. I was told that that year, Alan Robb won the Korkie Marathon in the morning and in the evening, he ran an easy five-kilometre jog around his neighbourhood.

> **APRIL 27**: *Set off intending to run ten kilometres, but after eight kilometres found myself stiffening up, so I shortened the run. Could still feel my Korkie Marathon effort.*

> **APRIL 28**: *Ran ten kilometres out towards Woodmead. My right shin was very painful. Rested, then ran five kilometres back home. Legs ached a bit but must push distance now.*

A common fear among all Comrades novices shortly after finishing a 50 – 56-kilometre ultra is that they will not cope with the extra distance at Comrades. They know that 56 kilometres were a bitter struggle, and they cannot imagine that they will cope with the additional 30 – 40 kilometres. They become quite despondent. I felt the same in 1977 after finishing the Korkie; I was delighted with my run in the Korkie, but it had been a very tough struggle, and my new friend Louis had dragged me through to the finish. Suddenly the Comrades challenge seemed insurmountable. If I had known then what I know now I would have reassured myself with the following major affirmations.

You will cope with the extra distance and the hills in the Comrades Marathon because:

1) You still have some serious training ahead of you. You will be stronger, fitter and leaner by race day.

2) You will be running the Comrades Marathon, the greatest race in South Africa and one of the world's most famous races. The Comrades is not like the

Korkie, which was a marathon run along a dusty, litter-strewn road in Kempton Park, watched by a handful of spectators. The Comrades has charisma, history, tradition, excitement, hundreds of other runners (these days, thousands), and tens of thousands of cheering spectators to carry you to the finish. The Comrades is endowed with a rich sense of purpose.

3) Most importantly, your brain will have wired its neurons to meet the challenge ahead. It will have slowly prepared itself for a 90-kilometre battle. For weeks, possibly months, you will have been programming and conditioning your brain to run 90 hilly kilometres under 12 hours so that on race morning, you can meet the challenge.

APRIL 29: *No run.*

APRIL 30: *A ten-kilometre run to end the month. Tomorrow, the "Big One".*

During the eleventh month since I started my training, I ran 345 kilometres – another big month for me and my first ultramarathon completed. I had also run a few training weeks, covering the Comrades distance or further in seven days.

May 1977

> **MAY 1:** *Club 45-mile run (72 km). At about 29 miles, I dropped out for a while because of severe instep and ankle pains. Worked on them for a while and then came back to run 42 of the 45 miles. Finished very strongly at the end. The Comrades is ten more miles!*

The Club 45-miler was a Wits tradition, usually run from someone's house in Johannesburg's Northern suburbs to beyond Sterkfontein and back. We were followed by a flotilla of vehicles driven by friends and spouses who stopped at agreed intervals to give us drinks and encourage us. Up to 100 Comrades hopefuls participated. We novices were motivated and counselled by experienced runners Dave Hodgskiss, Steve Alperstein and John Bush. We were encouraged to aim for "time on our feet" and not to be too concerned about the speed we covered those 45 miles. The run was, and still is, designed to get our legs accustomed to many hours of running. After that first long club run, I never again attempted to run 45 miles in one training run. In future years I would run between 60 – 65 kilometres, and I felt that was sufficient, and I always boasted, "I won't be completing this 45-miler". In future years I would also not make the mistake of racing a hard ultramarathon (the Korkie 53-kilometre) and then run 45 miles a week later. There was simply not enough time to recover. I was fortunate not to become injured after that ridiculous week. That was not intelligent thinking or planning. Ideally, very long runs should be spaced apart by intermediate shorter runs i.e.

First Sunday of the month: 53 kilometres.
Second Sunday of the month: 25 kilometres.
Third Sunday of the month: 65 kilometres.
Fourth Sunday of the month: 20 kilometres.
Fifth Sunday of the month: 30 kilometres.

WEEKLY MILEAGE:

Approximately 105 kilometres.

MAY 2: *No run. Rested.*

MAY 3: *Ran five kilometres at an easy pace.*

MAY 4: *Ran 13 fast kilometres. Some stretching before the run helped.*

Stretching before or after a run has always been a contentious matter for me. In later years I found I was often injured when I stretched (yes, perhaps I wasn't stretching correctly), but after a while, I dropped stretching from my pre-run routine and simply ran my opening couple of kilometres gently and then picked up the pace.

MAY 5: *Four miles (7 km) on my own. What a struggle. I battled the whole way. My legs were tight from the first mile and were then tight and sore.*

MAY 6: *No run.*

MAY 7: *No run.*

MAY 8: *A 25-mile run with the club. My legs were sore after ten miles, and I hobbled my way in over the last five miles. I have simply done too much since the Korkie. From now on I am cutting back for the Comrades.*

At least I recognised the problem.

WEEKLY MILEAGE:

Approximately 80 kilometres.

MAY 9: *Five-kilometre run. Very stiff and sore.*

MAY 10: *Seven-kilometre run. Felt good at the start, but I soon began to feel heavy and tired.*

MAY 11: *Seven-kilometre run again. Much better though I am still not 100%.*

MAY 12: *Ran January 10-route (10 km). Started out slow but found myself running faster and* *faster as the kilometres clicked by. Finished strongly in 37:40 after 41:00 in January.*

MAY 13: *No run.*

MAY 14: *No run.*

MAY 15: *No run.*

My experienced Wits teammates advised me to take a break from training for a few days. I had been complaining that I felt sluggish and heavy-legged on training runs and that I was permanently tired. In later years, my training partner, Graeme Lindenberg, would describe that leaden-legged feeling as the "plods". Later, we called the even heavier dead legs feeling when the warning from the "plods" is ignored, as the "super-plods".

WEEKLY MILEAGE:
Approximately 30 kilometres.

Coincidentally, my break from running was also triggered by meeting Annie, a lovely young lady who distracted me more than a little. (*Horror vacui* – nature abhors a vacuum.) Running was no longer the only important interest in my life, and running was now not the only therapy helping to heal my damaged heart.

> MAY 16: *A three-day layoff. I was feeling a bit jaded,*
> *and I wanted to give my legs a good rest. Ran a very*
> *enjoyable seven miles this morning in cool conditions.*
>
> MAY 17: *Fast nine miles (15 km) with the club at a*
> *fearsome pace up Jan Smuts Avenue. Felt good all the*
> *way. I am dreading an injury or a cold at this stage.*

Every Comrades runner becomes desperately worried at this stage. Barring a fall or an accident, injuries are not likely in the last couple of weeks before race day. Injuries usually strike earlier in the Comrades training build-up. However, infections are possible. I always avoided people who were ill and had an anti-flu vaccination early in the running season.

> MAY 18: *Fast seven miles (12 km) with the club, including*
> *the Westcliff Steps and a stretch on the Parkview Golf*
> *Course. Selected for the Wits A team for the cross-*
> *country race on Saturday. I am a bit apprehensive.*

My first cross-country race and I had every reason to be apprehensive. I never really mastered cross-country running or trail running when the sport started formally many years later. I think a combination of dodgy eyesight and a love for the security of the solid, stable road made me wary of the broken rhythm and bumpy surfaces of cross-country running. Nevertheless, in later years I improved and was a scoring team member when Wits twice won the Transvaal Cross-country Club Championships in the 1980s. I also noticed that Alan Robb ran every cross-country league race for his club, Germiston Callies, and he raced quite well. (He won the 1977 Comrades Marathon.)

> **MAY 19**: *Tough 15 miles (25 km) from Noel de Charmoy's house which included some gruesome climbs. I felt very relaxed for most of the run and led the bunch up the hills.*

Noel and Lian de Charmoy's post-run tea was always a highlight. Lian's pecan pie was simply scrumptious. Noel ran a sub-seven-hour silver Comrades in 1978 and in later years became one of my key seconds. The video of him handing me a bottle and shaking my hand on Washington Road in 1983 with three kilometres to go, remains a special moment. Noel and Lian went on to start parkrun in New Zealand.

> **MAY 20**: *No run. Resting.*

> **MAY 21**: *Frankenwald Cross-country Transvaal A-League 12-kilometre. Not one of my most memorable races. Was drained after a "heavy" night.*

Annie Freemantle. Annie died of cancer in 2010.
On a trek in Nepal that same year, I left her
photograph alongside one of my father, Noel, lying
in the snow on a pass of Manaslu Mountain. When I
turned to look back, a gust of wind had carried the
two photographs high up and almost out of sight
against the rocky slopes of the Himalayan giant.

I had been to a party with my new girlfriend Annie, and it was a wild and late one. Also drained after Noel's 15-miler. But those are poor excuses. I ran badly. Battled on the uphills and on the rough sandy sections on the course. Finished 44th out of 120, with Hamish and Dave Johnson both equally as disappointed as me. Jax finished 13th and was the first Witsie to reach the finish line. We were given a quarter of an orange to suck afterwards, and I was breathing so deeply I nearly swallowed mine in one gulp. Cross-country on the Highveld is always very tough. The thin, dusty air and hilly courses often laid out on old gold mine dumps make running very taxing.

This particular race may have been an unhappy experience for me that day, but the idea of a short, hard run a few days before the Comrades became a permanent part of my training programme for years to come. In later years a high placing in a cross-country race (top ten or a sub-thirty-minute ten-kilometre) told me everything I needed to know about my fitness and preparedness for the Comrades.

MAY 22: *No Run.*

> **WEEKLY MILEAGE:**
> **Approximately 75 kilometres.**

MAY 23: *Six-mile (10 km) run with the club.*

MAY 24: *Fifteen-mile (25 km) depleting run with Hamish and Jean to start Saltin diet. Hilly course, very fast pace. Feel drained.*

The Saltin diet (or Saltin-Hermansson diet to give it its full name) was used by a few runners in the 1970s and early 1980s and was supposed to give runners an extra edge in a marathon by extending each runner's "fuel tank". (Their muscle and liver glycogen stores were apparently boosted.) It was first used by Swedish long-distance skiers but was popularised by English marathon runner, Ron Hill. In the 1970s, Ron Hill was one of the world's leading marathon runners. For two years, 1970 and 1971, he was probably the world's number one marathoner. In that time, he won the Commonwealth Games and European Championship Marathon and became the first Briton to win the Boston

Marathon. He used the Saltin diet in all three races. Ron is also a scientist with a PhD in chemistry. It was his enquiring, scientific mind that led him to research papers and articles on human performance, and it was here that he discovered the diet. The Saltin diet is also known as the carbo-loading diet and the glycogen depletion diet. The objective of the diet is to overfill the carbohydrate tanks in the muscles by up to 125%, having first completely emptied them. A week before race day, runners complete a fast 25 – 30-kilometre run, in the process depleting the muscles of glycogen. For the next three days, they continue to train but exclude all carbohydrates from their diets. This further depletes the muscles and liver of glycogen. (Consider that in the 1970s none of us had heard of the Banting diet, L.C.H.F., Keto or Paleo. Indeed, even Tim Noakes, renowned scientist, sports medicine practitioner, and marathoner with over 70 marathons and ultramarathons to his credit, and whose book, *The Real Meal Revolution*, must be one of the most important books ever written would have carbo-loaded diligently for each of the seven Comrades Marathons he ran.) This "zero carbohydrates" part of the diet can be difficult to endure. (These days, as a fat-adapted, Banting follower I would find it a pleasure.) Running becomes progressively more difficult, and hills are very taxing. Each day running becomes harder, and some runners may even experience leg cramps. I found that on a couple of occasions on the third day of depletion, my muscles cramped. Runners can become irritable, dizzy and light-headed at times. Running a short distance like eight kilometres is a major challenge by the third day, and ninety kilometres appears to be out of the question. This is not an encouraging physical or psychological state to be in with the Comrades Marathon looming around the corner. As I became an experienced user of the Saltin diet, the worse I felt on the depletion part of the diet, the better I felt emotionally. I knew it was working as it was supposed to. However, it can take some intense persuasion to convince a newcomer to follow the diet. These symptoms are all excellent news, and on the fourth day, runners start a complete dietary turnaround and switch to consuming only carbohydrates while they cease all training. For three days, they rest and load with carbohydrates. The idea is that on race morning they line-up fresh, rested, and powered by a super overloaded fuel tank. I certainly felt fabulous when, on the third day, I started eating carbohydrates again. The Saltin diet was and still is very contentious. There were those who swore by it and those who detested it. I fell into the former category. After using the diet for my first Comrades, I relied on it for every single serious Comrades and major ultramarathon I raced after that. It became part of my pre-race ritual, and I swore by it. But in the word "ritual" lies a clue to my thinking. As an archaeology student, I understood the importance of ritual and in particular, the importance of ritual for Iron Age ironworkers. In order to smelt iron from broken chunks of iron ore so that they could fashion spearheads and other iron tools, Iron Age ironworkers followed a special ritual. Some parts of this ritual make perfect scientific sense, some of it does not. This included building a special smelting furnace often using termite mound soil, using large wooden bellows, charcoal and wood to heat the furnace to over 1100°C. But they also used rituals to encourage good iron production and to ward off bad spirits. These rituals included songs and prayers and various types of muti (traditional African medicine) which were buried under the furnace or placed into the furnace. There were also strict taboos such as ensuring that the furnace was constructed at a distance from the village and that all women were excluded from the process. These ironworkers knew that as long as they stuck to every part of the ritual, they would be able to smelt iron successfully. So, they never altered any part of the ritual. In the same way, I stuck to my ritual for every final week of preparation for every major race I ran from then on. Perhaps the Saltin diet worked its magic, or perhaps the enforced rest and pre-race taper were the answers, or perhaps it was my simmering mental state in those last days where I slowly prepared myself for battle, but whatever it was, for more than a decade I was able to smelt iron very successfully every time. (I did not banish women from my ritual.)

> MAY 25: *Six-mile run (10 km) with the club and guest, Alan Robb. Couldn't really feel the diet on day one.*

Alan Robb was a guest speaker at our club that evening, and he joined us for a run before the function. I remember staring at him as if at a ghost or an astronaut who had walked on the moon. Here was a man who had actually won the Comrades Marathon! I stood transfixed and tried desperately to spot whatever magic ingredient he had, but Alan was the quiet, modest Alan Robb he has always been. He was just a normal young man who ran incredibly well. A few days after appearing as a guest of honour and guest speaker at our club function, he won the 1977 "up" run in a new record time of 05:47. He would go on to win four times, including an incredible run in 1978 where he became the first runner to break the five and a half hour barrier, winning by twenty minutes. He also earned twelve gold medals for finishing in the top ten and has now run forty-two Comrades Marathons. In the years ahead, Alan and I were to become great running rivals and friends. Apart from our love of running and our mutual respect, we are almost polar opposites.

Alan is modest and humble. If you chatted to him all day and you didn't know him, you might never discover that he is a Comrades champion. It would take me about five minutes to tell you that I have won the Comrades. He is a passionate Liverpool football fan, hence his red socks and the floppy Liverpool hat which he wore in many Comrades Marathons. (I support Manchester United.) Although he won the 1977 "up" run, Alan really loves the "down" run. (He was to win the "down" run three times, and he was always much more dangerous as a competitor when running a "down" run). I am a great fan of the "up" run. By listening to Alan and watching how he trained, I was able to learn so much.

> MAY 26: *Five kilometres. Did not feel too bad but missing coffee with three spoons of sugar, ice cream and hot chocolate sauce, and a chocolate éclair.*
>
> MAY 27: *Five kilometres. Could feel the diet. I felt drained, and I lacked punch on the hills. Cramped quite badly once near the end.*

And that was my last run before the race itself. Many runners like to run right up to the morning of the race. They feel they get too lethargic and stodgy if they don't have at least one short run to stretch out their legs. I like to rest for all three days. In fact, I like that lethargic but pent-up feeling where I feel like a tightly wound spring waiting to unwind, a spring that I am going to release very gradually on race morning. I always shake my head in disbelief at runners hurtling up and down the Durban beachfront the day before the race. Are they checking to see if they feel fit and ready? What if they don't get the answer they were hoping for? Are they hoping this last run will squeeze in that last ounce of fitness or are they just showing off? "Hey, look at me, I'm running Comrades tomorrow". I urge every runner to simply rest for two or three days before the race!

> **MAY 28**: *No run. Carbohydrate loading.*
> *Broke the diet with two gooey jam doughnuts,*
> *a bar of chocolate and two beers.*

Now I realise how addicted I was to junk carbohydrates. I remember feeling elated, almost high when I swallowed those first carbohydrates. Now I would feel ill.

> **MAY 29**: *No run. Carbohydrate loading.*

I left Johannesburg late and drove to Ladysmith with my mate David who was going to second me in my first Comrades. I remember being so excited as the great adventure began. On the way, we passed other Comrades runners or were passed by them as everyone was making the journey to the great race. I stuck my Comrades numbers on the back window of my Hillman Arrow, and other runners hooted and waved their own numbers from their car windows. (In those days our numbers and a race programme were posted to us a few days before the race.)

David and I spent the night at the Crown Hotel in Ladysmith. This old hotel still stands and still welcomes Comrades runners each year. The hotel restaurant presented those old-style seven-course menus, starting with soup, then a mock prawn cocktail in pink mayonnaise, a fish dish, two meat dishes and a dessert, followed by a cheese platter. David and I tore through that and washed it all down with whisky and two bottles of red wine. (Well, I was carbohydrate loading!)

MAY 30: *No run. Carbohydrate loading.*

The day before the race. We drove to Pietermaritzburg where we met other running friends and then drove over the route. I believe that driving the Comrades route is one of the most important final acts of preparation for any Comrades runner. It is terrifying, and I understand why some runners argue that they prefer not knowing what lies ahead. These are the people who look away when the doctor is about to administer an injection. I prefer to look. I don't like nasty shocks. I insist on studying the Comrades route, particularly the major hills, and I pay plenty of attention to the last 20 kilometres.

Even when I was a veteran of over 20 Comrades Marathons, I drove over the route every year that I was running the marathon. In recent years I have conducted route tours for novices and foreign runners and the changing emotional responses of the runners on the tour is fascinating to watch. At first, as we embark on the tour, the runners are excited, jovial, behaving like children on a school outing to the zoo, where there will be ice cream. Later, as the drive progresses and the tour bus grinds its way up and down the Comrades hills, the bus grows quieter. It grows quieter still when someone enquires about the name of a long, steep hill the bus is battling to climb, and I reply that it has no name. "This is not one of the famous registered hills," I tell them. By the time we are approaching the finish, the passengers on the bus are silent. No one is excited anymore, and many runners are busy adjusting their pacing charts. No one is expecting to run a faster time than they had originally planned. As the runners disembark to walk the final lap in the finish stadium, I see furrowed brows, pale faces and I hear muted conversation. Everyone is concerned, if not downright scared; the route tour has served its purpose. You see, scared Comrades runners are successful Comrades runners. Scared runners start the race slowly and cautiously, and they use their reserves of energy sparingly. As I have emphasised earlier in this guide, the Comrades Marathon does not reward the bold and brave – it rewards the timid and meek.

(For information on joining my Comrades route tour, please check my website www.brucefordyce.com)

When I drove the Comrades route on May 30, 1977 (the day before the Comrades), I was terrified. It just seemed to go on and on and on, and the hills seemed endless. I remember being particularly haunted by Polly Shortts, which I described as a mineshaft (my first Comrades was an "up" run). The next morning, I ran very cautiously at the start and held myself in check for most of the first half. Though I lost about ten minutes in the second half, I did not slow down nearly as badly as those around me, and I found myself passing runners for most of the second half.

In those days there was no pre-race expo to attend. (Our numbers were posted to us before the race.) The next hurdle to be negotiated was the attempt to sleep the night before the race. I stayed with friends in Westville for that first run. In this modern era, I cannot recommend strongly enough staying in Durban or near surrounds for the "up" run and Pietermaritzburg or villages above Pietermaritzburg (Hilton, Howick or Midmar) for the "down" run. Normally, sleep comes easily to Comrades runners, but this is a warning to all Comrades novices – for a variety of reasons, sleep does not come easily, if at all, the night before the race:

1) You try to fall asleep in a strange bed in a strange room, with a lumpy pillow and a persistent mosquito dive-bombing you.

2) You have rested and tapered for race day. You simply aren't tired ... at all.

3) You are so nervous and excited that thousands of butterflies are zooming around your stomach. You close your eyelids, but underneath them, your eye-balls are wide open.

4) Your partner or running mate is tossing and turning or snoring next to you or in the other bed.

5) As you start to drift off, you realise your bladder is full.

When you do finally drift off, you will wake again with a start, and a pounding heart at 03:00. After that, sleep is impossible.

The veterans told me that sleep the night before the race is not critical. It is the night before the night before that getting a good night's sleep becomes important. (And of course, the amusing question that gets asked every year: Is there anything wrong with having sex the night before the Comrades? The answer: If you can get it, there is nothing wrong at all, it's just staying up all night looking for sex that is a problem.)

I always found the day before the race a long, slow, boring day full of anxious moments and worry. You will find yourself glancing at your watch at frequent intervals and wandering where you will be at the same time the next day. I used to pin my race numbers on my vest and lay out my running gear in my hotel room. Our numbers were made of light cotton in those days, and some runners sewed their numbers onto their vests. The number could make a handy pocket if the top was left unstitched and open. Runners crammed their essential items and supplies into this pocket. Though my teammate, Mike Applewhite, considered a packet of Marie biscuits, cigarettes and matches essential items. After that, there wasn't too much to do except enjoy a last carbohydrate meal, and when I stayed in the old Royal Hotel, stare out of my hotel room window and watch the tide in the harbour drifting in and out every few hours.

MAY 31: *THE COMRADES MARATHON! What a great race. I have never run so far or so hard for so long in my life. It was 90 kilometres of hard climbing. I was hoping for any time between seven and seven and a half hours (silver medal) and to finish inside the top 100. I am delighted with 43ʳᵈ place in 06:45. There was a massive field of 2 212. I didn't find the early climbing too hard. Cruised up Field's Hill and Botha's Hill. Legs started to get sore on the descent to Drummond. Despite being*

147

10 to 15 minutes ahead of schedule at halfway, I managed to maintain the pace, and I was catching runners in the second half. Inchanga Hill was tough but not too bad. I started to struggle from Camperdown onwards. Went up Mpusheni (Little Polly's) in a daze. Struggled up to Ashburton village. Ran a quarter of Polly Shortts, and then walked 50 metres, ran 50 metres to the top. Lost a minute or so up Polly Shortts. Very quick last kilometre into Jan Smuts Stadium. Finished 3rd Witsie in 06:45 behind teammates Hamish (18th) and Graeme (19th). Now I have a beautiful silver medal, a Comrades badge and very, very stiff legs.

The only decent photograph I have from my first Comrades. Climbing Inchanga Hill with Les Wilton.

My 1977 Comrades Marathon silver medal and badge.

And so I became a Comrades runner! A dream that started on a cold winter night a year before became a reality. That day is indelibly etched into my mind. It will be for you too when you run your first Comrades. It was both the longest and the shortest day of my life. It was a day in which I ran the full gamut of emotions from despair to joy, from anger to happiness, weakness to strength. I remember the noise and turmoil at the start and the war cry we Witsies belted out before the starting gun. The noise from hundreds of runners was nearly drowned out by the chirping of thousands of Indian mynah birds that were calling from the floodlit trees. There was no playing of "Chariots of Fire". (The movie hadn't been made yet and Vangelis was not to

compose his famous piece until 1981.) There was no national anthem, and no "Shosholoza". We did listen to Max
Trimborn's cockerel crow, belted out by Max himself. He
was still alive in 1977.

The modern 21st century Comrades Marathon start is
quite easily the most emotional and inspiring marathon
start in the world and has become an essential part of the
Comrades experience.

There was a brief moment before the starting gun when
I realised that this is it. This is the culmination of months
of training. This is the start of the Comrades Marathon,
and you are about to run it. Then we were off, and I recall
constantly having to rein myself in and to resist the urge to
"go". Even so, I was ahead of schedule from early on.

I remember the early morning warmth and the sweat
on the runners' backs as we toiled up the Berea. I can recall
my teammate, John Bush, saying, "It's hot guys. It's going
to be a tough one." Then it just seemed like a never-ending
climb. I recall my father jumping into the road in Pinetown
and cheering me on. Later, at Alverstone, I passed the
same two Springs Striders runners who had encouraged
me at my very first race. "You've improved a lot, Witsie,"
one commented.

On the dreadful Harrison Flats, I kept asking myself
why I was doing this. At Umlaas Road I can recall seeing
Polly Shortts shimmering in the heat, a pale blue ridge in
the distance.

I was hanging on, and in a daze running down to the bridge
at Tumble Inn, Mpusheni (Little Polly's), when I heard
a spectator's radio announcing, "Here comes race leader
Alan Robb into the stadium and my goodness doesn't he

look fresh and strong and full of running". That was quite a low moment for me as about 12 kilometres and two of the toughest hills of the "up" run still lay in front of me.

I asked Alan to write me his account of the 1977 Comrades. In addition to winning the race that morning, he also broke the record, but in typical very modest Alan Robb style this is what he gave me:

Running with Alan Robb in 1982 – I was
an hour behind him in 1977.

"UP" RUN 1977 – Alan Robb

After winning the Comrades in 1976, my training and racing continued to go well. During 1977 I won the Korkie Marathon, was second in the Interprovincial Marathon Championships and sixth in the Two Oceans. I ran a p.b. of 1 hour, 45 minutes at the Spring Striders 32-kilometre race. I ran regular eight-kilometre time trials in about 26 minutes. For those who know Johannesburg, the road to the Top Star Drive-in, and Sylvia Pass were my favourite hills for hill training.

The Favourite

I started the race as one of the favourites along with a host of Natal runners such as Steve Atkins, Dave Rogers, Norman Wessels and Dave Wright. Everyone was punting Vincent Rakabaele as the first black runner to win the Comrades. At the last moment, 1974/75 champion, Derek Preiss withdrew with an injury.

The Run

I started the race feeling good and ran with all the contenders. Dave Wright went into the lead in Pinetown and built up a three-minute lead at half-way (02:52) which was slower than the previous "up" run. Rakabaele and I then upped the pace and ran stride by stride, catching and passing Dave Wright. At Mpushini, Rakabaele suddenly started slowing down, which left me with a comfortable run to the finish to win by ten minutes. It was one of those few races where you can say that everything went well. The harder training paid off, especially the hill work I did because I am not the greatest hill runner.

My own finish ended almost an hour later in a confused blur of cheering crowds and four or five runners sprinting next to me. I don't remember too much except that as I passed under the finish banner, I flung my headband into the air. My legs collapsed beneath me and looking around for support, I fell into my father's arms and hugged him. He hugged me back, and held me up until I had recovered and my legs had stopped trembling.

Afterwards, it occurred to me that that was the first time I had ever hugged my father. Not that he didn't love me, nor I him, but we didn't hug. We normally shook hands. Occasionally he might place a hand on my shoulder. Officers in the British army did not hug their sons or other men. They shook hands.

A few years later he wrote me a special letter that I still treasure. In it he told me how proud he was to be my father. "Thanks to you," he wrote, "people now know how to pronounce our surname." In the old days he found it simpler to book a restaurant table or leave a telephone message using the name "Ford". He ended the letter so informally: "With all my love, Dad". And then he added: "P.S. Isn't it interesting how you earned your own medals."

I thought of how this veteran soldier who had earned campaign medals fighting on the border between Hong

Kong and China and in the jungles of Brunei, The Malayan Peninsula, Sarawak and Borneo must, at one stage, have been a little concerned about the direction his long-haired slightly built, partying son was taking. He concluded: "It takes a special kind of valour to earn a Comrades medal."

Like all Comrades runners, I vowed that I would never run the race again. I sat down with my family and just stared at my feet in a daze for several minutes afterwards. All my toenails were blue, and they were aching.

Later I sat in the bath in my room for over an hour watching the occasional drip from the tap make small ripples on the surface as the water grew colder and colder and my fingers became wrinkled with granny skin. I realised that I would never be the same person that I had been before the race. The part of old me had died on the Comrades road, and like Hermes, I had crossed into another world. I would be a bolder, more determined person. I had changed forever. You will too when you complete this journey from your old world to your new world. And like most Comrades runners, I changed my mind I knew I would have to run this remarkable race again.

As the sun was setting over the Jan Smuts (now Harry Gwala) Stadium on the evening of my first Comrades Marathon, I heard the plaintive ringing tone of a lone bugle. It drifted across the field over the heads of hundreds of exhausted runners, many sprawled like war-dead on the dry winter grass. I recognised the tune. The bugler was playing "The Last Post". Many Comrades runners, but particularly novices, may not understand why "The Last Post" is played at the end of each Comrades Marathon. It is played to signify the end of the day's activities but is also sounded at military funerals and commemorative services. The haunting notes of "The Last Post" remind us of the reasons Vic Clapham started the race in 1921 and why it is called "The Comrades Marathon". I think Hermes would approve.

Glossary

Alverstone: A huge radio/communications mast that is visible from the Comrades route. The SABC used to broadcast the race from studios below Alverstone Tower.

Ancel Keys, whose "healthy diet" and demonisation of cholesterol and fat, turned out to have been one of the greatest lies in modern medical history and helped to kick-start the obesity pandemic in the USA. His research was exposed as gravely flawed by Tim Noakes and many other scientists.

Ashburton: A small village at the top of Little Polly's, Mpusheni. A major milestone on the "up" run – just over ten kilometres left to run.

Banting diet: A modern Keto and low carbohydrate diet named after William Banting, who used a diet low in carbohydrates to deal with his corpulence. Popularised Tim Noakes.

Biltong: Dried and cured meat from venison or beef. A national snack in Southern Africa and also used in stews, baked goods, etc. A bit like American jerky but much nicer.

Blown: The dead feeling runners endure when they have hit the wall and are reduced to a slow shuffle. As in, "He's blown. You'll catch him now".

Braaivleis (Braai): Traditional South African barbeque but far nicer! Featuring traditional boerewors (sausage) and large quantities of beer. Hundreds of spectators at Comrades "braai" while watching the race, also, after major victories at rugby matches. Only South Africans smelling the tell-tale aroma of boerewors cooking say, "Ah, someone's having a braai".

Bail: To drop out of the race (unthinkable in the Comrades). Like, "Bail out of the aeroplane". Usually encountered straight after "blowing".

Botha's Hill: Steep and winding climb just before Botha's Hill village on the "up" run. Considered one of the major registered hills in the Comrades and signals the beginning of the downhill drop to the Indian Ocean on the "down" run.

Bryanston: An affluent, residential suburb of Sandton, just north of Johannesburg.

Durban: The largest city in the province of KwaZulu-Natal and the third-largest city in South Africa, boasting the busiest port. Named in 1835 after Sir Benjamin D'Urban, governor of the Cape.

Fields Hill: At close to four kilometres, Field's is the longest hill in the Comrades Marathon and one of the five registered hills. (The others being Cowie's Hill, Botha's Hill, Inchanga and Polly Shortts.) Encountered quite early in the race (23 kilometres or so and considered a good litmus test for how a runner will cope with the rest of the "up" run. Very painful on the "down" run. Bone-jarring descent. On a clear day, it is possible to glimpse the Indian Ocean from the summit of Fields.)

Harrison Flats: A long, flat stretch about 33 kilometres from the end of the "up" run. Very dull, burned, boring brown veld scattered with litter. The road ahead drops slightly downhill on the "up" run, and it is possible to make up time, but it is grim running. This is the "never, ever again" stretch of the race.

Inchanga: Zulu for "blade of a knife". A long, steep and winding climb encountered immediately after half-way. (Drummond village.) Very hard going.

Mpusheni (Little Pollys): In my opinion the most mentally taxing hill in the "up" run of the Comrades Marathon. Would be as difficult as Polly Shortts itself but has a slight dip and flat section a third of the way up which offers some respite. Encountered about 12 kilometres from the end, it warns every runner how tough the real Polly Shortts will be. Invariably mistaken for Polly Shortts by novice runners.

Northcliff: A Residential suburb of Johannesburg on the Northcliff Ridge with lovely views of Johannesburg.

Parkrun: parkruns are free, weekly, five-kilometre community events all over the world which takes place on Saturdays in parks and open spaces. They are positive, encouraging and inclusive. The concept was created by Paul Sinton-Hewitt, who seconded me on occasion in the Comrades Marathon and were introduced to my wife Gill and me in April 2011. Paul asked us to start parkruns in South Africa, and our first parkrun took place in Johannesburg's Delta Park in November 2011. Twenty-six people attended. Since then, we have grown to 225 parkruns with 1.2 million registered members. When I ran those first steps in June 1976, I had no idea that an event I would run nearly 40 years later would have as much significance for me as the Comrades Marathon itself.

Pietermaritzburg: The capital of the province of KwaZulu-Natal and the second-largest city in the province. Named after Voortrekker leaders Piet Retief and Gerrit Maritz and established in 1838.

Polly Shortts: A famous hill near the end of the Comrades "up" run, about nine kilometres from the finish. Very tough 1.8-kilometre climb with several deceptive bends. Named after the farmer, Portland Bentinck Shortts, who lived there at the turn of the last century. His farm was situated about a mile from the old Star and Garter Pub which stood 25 yards outside the Pietermaritzburg municipal boundary and was, therefore, able to sell liquor on Sundays. Mr Shortts loved his whisky.

Seconds: Person or persons who assist a runner along the road by bringing drinks, sponges or information. Also yell encouragement and lies, "You're looking great", or "You're nearly there". Called a "pacer" in the USA.

Shosholoza: A traditional miners' song sung in Zulu and Ndebele, meaning "go forward", or "make way." Some parts are reminiscent of a steam train. It is considered South Africa's second national anthem. Sung shortly before the start of the race.

Soweto: English syllabic abbreviation for **So**uth **We**stern **To**wnships. Formerly, a township for black South African migrant labourers for Johannesburg's gold mines.

Umlaas Road: The highest point on the Comrades route despite the fact that Polly Shortts still looms ahead on the "up" run. Some joke will invariably shout, "Downhill all the way from here!"

Vasbyt: An Afrikaans word for "endure" but much stronger. When its really tough and everything hurts, you have to "byt vas". Pronounced as if the "v" is an "f."

Witsie: A student from Johannesburg's University of the Witwatersrand. (South Africa's finest university.) Pronounced as if the "w" is a "v."

FordyceFusion

It is impossible to describe how much pleasure I have derived from sharing my love of running with so many people through the Comrades, road races and parkrun, but despite this, I have been frustrated by my inability to reach out and provide the personal guidance so many have asked for to help them make the most of their efforts.

Through my books, I have enjoyed sharing my running knowledge, ideas, and experiences, but have been acutely aware that each runner is unique and therefore requires guidance based on their personal goals, genetics, performance etc. The "no man's land" between general and specific personalised training advice needed to be addressed.

I'm therefore delighted to announce that the publication of this book coincides with the introduction of *FordyceFusion* (www.fordycefusion.com), which offers personal guidance for your running journey.

I hope you find this useful.